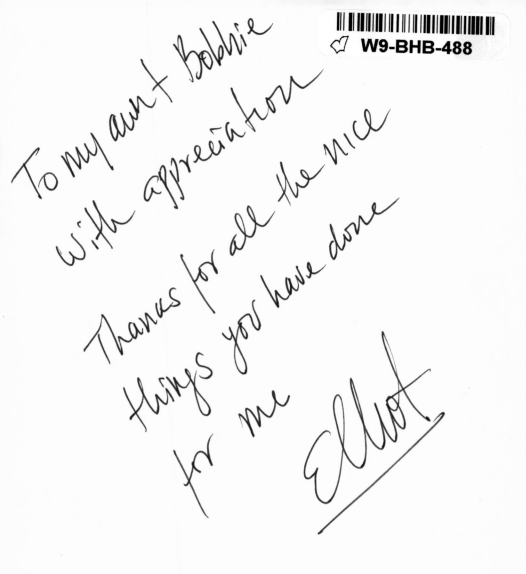

To my aunt Bobbie
with appreciation

Thanks for all the nice
things you have done

for me

Elliot

Logistics and the Extended Enterprise

Wiley Operations Management Series for Professionals

Other published titles in this series are:

Logistics and the Extended Enterprise

BENCHMARKS AND BEST PRACTICES
FOR THE MANUFACTURING PROFESSIONAL

Sandor Boyson

Thomas M. Corsi

Martin E. Dresner

Lisa H. Harrington

With

Elliot Rabinovich

John Wiley & Sons, Inc.

New York ➤ Chichester ➤ Weinheim ➤ Brisbane ➤ Singapore ➤ Toronto

This publication is designed to provide accurate and authoritative information in regard to the subject matter covered. It is sold with the understanding that the publisher is not engaged in rendering legal, accounting, or other professional services. If legal advice or other expert assistance is required, the services of a competent professional person should be sought.

Library of Congress Cataloging-in-Publication Data

Logistics and the extended enterprise: best practices for the
    manufacturing professional / Sandor Boyson ... [et al.].
      p. cm.—(Wiley operations management series for
    professionals)
      Includes index.
      ISBN 0-471-31430-7 (alk. paper)
      1. Business logistics—Cost effectiveness. 2. Delivery of
    goods—Management. 3. Industrial procurement. 4. Contracting
    Out.
      I. Boyson, Sandor. II. Series.
      HD38.5.L637 1999
      658.5—dc21   98-33306
                                                        CIP

Printed in the United States of America.
10 9 8 7 6 5 4 3 2 1

Contents

Preface

This book is the result of a four-year, $1 million research project devoted to the study of best practices in logistics (also called supply-chain management). It is dedicated to answering one question of profound importance to business and governments worldwide as we enter the new millennium: How can organizations best use logistics/supply-chain management practices to break down internal and external walls and become more effective extended enterprises?

Over 600 companies across a broad range of industries shared their experiences in supply-chain reengineering with our team of university and industry specialists from the Supply Chain Management Center at the R. H. Smith School of Business, University of Maryland. Through interviews, site visits, focus groups, and targeted surveys, we gained first-hand insights into the tremendous challenges and opportunities facing these companies as they sought to manage purchasing, transportation, warehousing, and order management/customer service processes in a new and integrated way.

Our team was fortunate indeed to have mounted a large-scale and well-funded research project at a time when the corporate role, mission, and technology of supply-chain management was in such deep, even radical flux. We have had a privileged vantage point from which to track the stupendous birth and emergence of the extended enterprise.

The structure and layout of our book is in two conceptual parts:

Part One, which encompasses Chapters 1 through 5, presents our framework for the best practices in logistics/supply-chain management. It covers the definition and evolution of the extended enterprise, the management of internal logistics/supply-chain practices; and the management of strategic supply-chain partnerships and outsourcing initiatives. It summarizes our core research findings and illustrates these findings with case studies.

Part Two, which encompasses Chapters 6 through 8, provides a diagnostic instrument for the reader to use in preparing a baseline assessment of his or her own organization's supply-chain practices, and a methodology to interpret and use the results of this diagnostic for supply-chain management improvement.

It is our hope that this book will provide the reader with both the conceptual and analytic tools necessary to master a holistic, integrative orientation to supply-chain management.

Finally, the authors would like to express their deep appreciation to the following individuals who have made many contributions to the research and preparation of this book. Elliot Rabinovich, PhD candidate at the R. H. Smith School of Business and our primary research assistant for the entire project. Elliot served as a contributing author. We could not have produced this book without his invaluable assistance. Larry Blalock, Ella McNeil, Richard Brancato and Jim Shuler of the U.S. Department of Energy, whose financial and moral support was so crucial throughout this project. Joseph Catto, Steen Carstensen, Randy Speight, Marvin

Crane, and John Buck, whose industry perspectives guided our thinking. Richard Mintz, whose policy perspectives helped us get through roiling waters. Tom Mierzwa, Alan Salton, Mike Mejza, and Mike Knemeyer, whose assistance and hard work were crucial inputs. Howard Frank, Judy Olian, and Curt Grimm, whose collegial support we have so gratefully received. And most of all to our spouses (Margarita, Sue, Lorrie, and Steve) and our families for responding with all their love and empathy during difficult periods of work.

Part I

Strategic Concepts and Best Practices

Logistics/Supply-Chain Management: The Hub of the Extended Enterprise

Logistics/supply-chain management is the synchronized movement of inputs and outputs in the production and delivery of goods and services to the customer. In this integrative approach, a cross-functional senior management group coordinates physical and informational resources to optimize efficiency and effectiveness. It manages both the purchasing (or inputs) side of the resource stream, and the distribution (or outputs) side of the stream as a single integrated flow. This flow typically encompasses customer service, physical distribution, materials management, information management, and their related, highly complex subprocesses: order processing and order tracking, production planning and supplier management, purchasing, warehousing, transportation, and electronic supply-chain communications/payment systems. Taken together, total supply chain costs consume about 7 to 12 percent of corporate annual revenue across all industries. In one year alone

(1997), U.S. corporations spent $862 billion on supply-chain activities, according to Cass Information Services' *1998 State of Logistics Report.*

Today, senior executives in many industries are managing extraordinarily complex global supply chains that source raw materials from thousands of locations around the world and distribute finished products to thousands of other locations. Many of these executives have come to recognize that corporate capability in supply-chain management is an important lever of enterprise transformation. This critical coordination and value center can enable the enterprise to synchronize many simultaneously unfolding material and informational flows on a worldwide basis—and help the whole enterprise to contain costs through more efficient utilization of assets and greater overall productivity.

As a result, integrated supply-chain management is now at the epicenter of business transformation. It has been elevated to the position of a hub, a crosscutting communications and strategic control nexus encompassing the major functional areas of the organization and the extended enterprise. A recent survey conducted by the University of Maryland Supply Chain Management Center found that 20 percent of Fortune 500 companies now have chief logistics officers (CLOs) reporting directly to the CEO—clear evidence of this area's growing stature as a critical lever of corporate transformation.

Chief logistics officers (and the even more powerful next generation of vice presidents of supply chain that are succeeding them) are breaking down walls between internal functions or departments, as well as between the enterprise itself and key partners in the value chain (e.g., customers, distributors, suppliers, and carriers). The very term "extended enterprise" refers to breaking down a company's outer wall and extending its strategy, structure, and processes to its core partners. The goal is to get everyone in the extended enterprise onto a common platform of logistics transactions and information systems for greater interorganizational "seamlessness." This integration can result in significantly faster system response times to volatile changes in marketplace events and patterns of demand. By creating and managing a highly organized network of complementary companies across the supply chain, an extended enterprise can also rapidly build strategic effectiveness and wealth.

This chapter describes the evolution and characteristics of a well-designed, well-managed extended enterprise, and it reviews corporate experience in achieving progressively greater integration with internal departments, suppliers, distributors, and customers. In doing so, it provides a tool for assessing your own company's stage of supply-chain development. Finally, the chapter concludes with a discussion of future trends that will enable expanded integration and even greater competitive benefits.

■ EVOLUTION AND CHARACTERISTICS OF THE EXTENDED ENTERPRISE

While the extended enterprise model may seem revolutionary, major elements of it are not new at all. They hearken back over a century to another time of radical technological and economic change. In his 1922 text, *The Industrial and Commercial Revolutions in Great Britain During the Nineteenth Century,* L. C. A. Knowles described the role of logistics in wealth creation in ways startlingly similar to the situation today:

> *Mechanical and rapid transport (railways and steamships) not merely altered the relative value of nations and commodities but it promoted a commercial revolution in business organization. As traders could get goods swiftly and with absolute certainty, they no longer kept such huge stocks. They therefore needed less*

warehousing space and less credit from their bankers and were able to carry on business more economically.

This sounds very much like the just-in-time inventory management practiced today, just as Knowles' description of the telegraph-enabled extended supply chains of the late 1800s sounds much like today's emerging IT-enabled extended supply chains:

> *It is now possible to control world-wide interests as one great business undertaking. The result is the formation of combinations that make for efficiency in production and the control of waste. It is possible to specialize branch factories to a very high degree, and raw material bought in large quantities is bought cheaper and is easier and less costly to handle. These combinations can obtain lower railway rates for their large shipments. They are also able to distribute from the nearest place of business and so save the expense of long railroad hauls. Businesses of this magnitude, national and international in scope, could not be carried on without daily correspondence to keep the whole in touch. They are therefore dependent for their existence on telegraphs and telephones.*

In the modern era, we can track the genesis of extended enterprise logistics to the early 1980s, when a new model of organization more appropriate for the hypercompetitive international marketplace began to surface. In the manufacturing sector, Japanese automobile makers began building factories with flexible automation capable of producing multiple types of products on the same production line. Instead of pushing large-volume, standardized production runs to reap economies of scale as was the common industrial practice in the West, Japanese firms engineered a lean and just-in-time manufacturing paradigm that sought big gains from economies of scope. The Japanese built fast-response production and logistics systems that could satisfy the pull of diverse and highly fluctuating international consumer demands.

A 1994 study by Nishiguchi[1] found that Japanese auto manufacturers throughout the 1980s maintained inventory levels one-fifteenth the size of European auto manufacturers and one-quarter the size of U.S. auto manufacturers. They also used just-in-time deliveries with 12 and five times greater frequency respectively than European and U.S. auto makers.

Soon, lagging American car manufacturers began to emulate Japanese practice, ordering key suppliers to move within 50 miles of plants to create greater synchronization in production. General awareness rapidly increased in Corporate America, which rushed to establish new, more responsive business models that were highly integrated horizontally and vertically across internal departments and external suppliers.

More recently, Japanese and American auto companies have begun to extend this integration into the dealer-support end of their business, using electronic sales information to guide continual parts-replenishment strategies. Honda Corporation has led the way among Japanese multinationals by constructing an international logistics network that unites country-specific local car dealerships, regional parts warehouses, and corporate headquarters in Tokyo into a single information system. This approach enables the company to maintain extremely low inventory stocks and conduct its customer service operations on an extremely fast turnaround basis.

By the early 1990s, this new approach to management had spread well beyond Japan and beyond the manufacturing sector. Service hierarchies were also transforming themselves into flexible global networks through telecommunications and electronic links of all kinds with suppliers and customers. By the late 1990s, a great wave of manufacturing and service businesses were moving to "network" models of organization, and many companies were establishing corporate logistics/supply-chain management hubs to provide information, resources, and guidance to keep networks functioning on an optimal basis. For example, to leverage corporatewide relationships and support both internal and external operating units, Xerox created strategic shared-service hubs at corporate headquarters to support areas like purchasing and technology where economies of scale and knowledge still made a big difference.

Today, supply-chain management, with its tendency to span functional boundaries and interact with many internal and external players, has become the driving force in the effort to create the extended enterprise. The supply-chain organization acts as the *body* of the enterprise, generating the dynamic energy and direction needed for the extended-enterprise network to operate efficiently and exchange inputs and outputs within its systemwide borders. It also acts as the *mind* of the extended enterprise, with computer software tracking the expanding physical production/distribution network map and applying optimization principles to restructure and streamline the network. Finally, at a more profound level, the supply-chain organization acts as the corporate survival instinct, with physical and informational supply lines branching out to secure vital corporate inputs like underground roots searching out water.

Typically, the logistics/supply-chain organizational hub has capabilities in customer order management, intermodal and international transportation management, information/data networking across the supply chain with vendors and customers, and performance/metrics management. It sells its services to the operating business units, and the units contribute to the budget of the logistics shared service on a utilization basis. In return, the units get purchasing discounts, lower operating costs, and higher levels of service from outside logistics/supply-chain actors than they could attain by operating alone.

The greater synchronization of production, distribution, and customer order management activities often brings dramatic gains. Work in process and finished goods inventory are slashed; order-to-delivery cycle times are compressed. In fact, best-in-class leaders in supply-chain management can have a 50 percent cost advantage over median competitors. According to a 1997 supply chain benchmarking study[2], conducted by The Performance Measurement Group, a subsidiary of global management consulting firm Pittiglio Rabin Todd & McGrath (PRTM), best in class companies:

➤ Enjoy an advantage in total supply chain management cost of 3–6 percent of revenue

➤ Hold 50–80 percent less inventory than their competitors

➤ Have a 40–65 percent advantage in cash-to-cash cycle time over average companies

"For a company with annual sales of $500 million and a 60 percent cost of sales, the difference between being at median in terms of [supply chain] performance and being in the top 20 percent is $44 million of available working capital," says PRTM director Mike Aghajanian.

What gives best-in-class companies these advantages? They have a holistic supply chain orientation, culture, and practices that allow them to see the entire set of activities from supply points to production points to warehouse/distribution points to the customer as one cross-functional, integrated process. Their constant priority is to eliminate handoff times and process disconnects across the supply chain.

Of course, firms do not attain best-in-class status overnight. The evolution many companies have experienced appears in the four stages of supply-chain evolution outlined in Figure 1.1. These stages of supply-chain management competency track the rise in stature, mission

Stage 1 Stunted Logistics Performer	Stage 2 Neophyte Logistics Performer	Stage 3 Internally Integrated Performer	Stage 4 Externally Integrated Logistics Performer
Logistics buried at lowest levels of corporate organizations.	Stovepiped logistics; each function acts in relative autonomy (e.g., purchasing decisions are detached from transportation or warehousing decisions). In addition, each operating unit or strategic business unit acts separately. There is an unsegmented supply base with no formal supply-chain partnerships.	Internal cross-functional teams spanning physical distribution functions such as transportation, warehousing, and customer order management; the start of segmenting the supply base and organizing core suppliers.	Intercorporate networked logistics teams and shared performance management information systems enable the corporation to manage its web of supply-chain relationships more in real time. Far closer alignment between production/service logistics and patterns of actual customer demand.
Logistics defined as shipping function.	Logistics defined as shipping and warehousing functions.	Logistics defined as shipping, warehousing, and customer service functions.	Logistics defined as total supply-chain integration: purchasing, shipping, warehousing, customer service, and collaborative planning/ forecasting functions.
Run by shipping clerks with little authority outside the immediate shipping area.	Run by military-style logisticians who exercise more authority to monitor performance of processes across a limited lateral span of control and take a range of improvement actions.	Run by a chief logistics officer with a high level of formal control over a greater lateral span of related logistics functions.	Run by a VP for supply chain with determinate strategic influence over supply-chain functions conducted by both internal operating units and externally owned operating units.

Figure 1.1 Stages of organizational growth in supply-chain management competency.

criticality, and reach of supply-chain management across and beyond the borders of the enterprise. (It is an extremely useful exercise to situate your own organization along this spectrum.)

Other supply-chain researchers also have documented this pattern of evolution. Masters and Pohlen[3] provided a chronological context for this development, noting that management styles have changed over time. While functional management was the dominant mode of the 1960s through 1970s, the 1980s moved to internal integration and the 1990s to external integration. Thus, companies who manage logistics on a functional basis are still mired in the 1970s and are some 30 years behind current best practices. Those who manage logistics well across the enterprise but who neglect to manage extended-enterprise relationships with the same intensity and effectiveness are at least 10 years behind current best practice. Even those companies that are high performers with unified management approaches across the entire chain cannot afford to rest, because revolutionary economic and technological forces continue to accelerate the pace of change.

■ FUTURE TRENDS IN SUPPLY-CHAIN MANAGEMENT

Full-spectrum visibility and real-time management of increasingly complex, high-velocity operations will be landmark practices of supply-chain management in the twenty-first century. These practices are already taking shape in organizations of all kinds.

For example, Ford Motor Company has opened its intranet to core suppliers so they can access real-time information on inventories in Ford plants and warehouses and engage in continual replenishment supply relationships. This intense logistics coordination is enabling suppliers to send a shipment of car seats packed so precisely that blue seats can be uncrated at the seat-installation station on the assembly line just as blue cars reach that station.

Or take the tactical control centers of the U.S. Army. At these centers, a logistician faces a wraparound 3D-control panel that provides "complete situational awareness." This panel shows the position of the tanks and soldiers on the battlefield. It shows—with total real-time visibility—supplies and material flowing into the frontlines of battle from regional theater locations and from staging areas around the world. It uses computer technology to locate additional suppliers instantly as needed and arrange new orders.

Using such state-of-the-art technology, the military is creating a network-centric global logistics environment characterized by unprecedented speed and agility. Perhaps this endeavor will spin off revolutionary new technologies and modes of management practice to the private sector in the years ahead. The military, which gave birth to the science of logistics in the Industrial Age, could well define the new supply-chain management paradigm of the Information Age.

We are only beginning to understand the revolutionary potential of these accelerating developments in supply-chain management. In fact, as we survey the millennial landscape, we can start to identify a whole series of converging forces and newly emerging capabilities that will surely shape the way extended-enterprise supply chains develop in the future. These include:

➤ Total real-time connectivity among extended-enterprise partners and deployment of ultrafast global information exchange networks within an increasingly open standard operating environment based on Internet protocols.

➤ A more holistic, systems-engineering and integration approach to value-chain management and more precise methods of costing and controlling transaction flows, such as *activity-based costing* and *business process reengineering.*

➤ The rapid rise of single-source, global third-party logistics companies that manage entire supply chains.

➤ The increased use of intermodal transportation for international and domestic shipping.

➤ The growing availability of computer-based government trade facilitation systems that ease import/export movements and enhance corporate supply-chain visibility and seamlessness.

The following sections discuss how each of these critical trends will condition the growth of extended-enterprise logistics.

➤ Total Connectivity

Information technology and telecommunications have catalyzed and accelerated the shift to the fully extended enterprise. The rise of corporate workgroup computing (e.g., PCs and LANs) led to high-performance work teams from the late 1980s to the early 1990s. In the mid-1990s, enterprisewide computing and the integration of key financial and operational databases led to more flexible internal structures. In the late 1990s, we have witnessed the rapid emergence of a seamless extended enterprise driven by leaps in information and telecommunications technologies.

In particular, the emergence of the Internet as the global information infrastructure backbone has accompanied the globalization of markets. It has given companies even greater tools for tightly orchestrating relationships across the entire value chain and creating strategic partnerships and operational linkages with a dynamic web of large and small firms spanning all continents. Internet-enabled shared information helps break down organization politics and functional fences, helping supply-chain alliance members develop a common understanding of the competitive environment. Presumably, all companies—suppliers, customers, and third parties—can benefit from a more open information flow by using the information to:

➤ Reduce or eliminate unnecessary inventory

➤ Improve their planning

➤ Develop active rather than reactive operations

➤ Smooth product flows

➤ Trim cost

➤ Improve service

These benefits will increase as the pace of the global knowledge revolution and the diffusion of technological infrastructure accelerate. The Internet's multimedia interface, the World Wide Web—and the growing pervasiveness of Web-enabled electronic commerce applications of all kinds—will certainly strengthen and become the strategic "anchor" forces in the global technological environment.

A 1998 White House report on electronic commerce describes the quickening pace of Web development and access in the United States.

The wait for broadband Internet access to households is measured in years not decades. Within the next five to 10 years, the vast majority of Americans should be able to interact with the Internet from their television sets, watch television on their PCs, and make telephone calls from both devices. These combined services will be brought to homes by satellite, wireless, microwave, tele-

vision cable and telephone lines all interconnected in one overall system.[4]

It would be incorrect to assume that Internet architecture is limited to North America or Europe. The *New York Times* reported recently that 10.48 percent of people in Hong Kong were already using the Internet; in Singapore, the estimate is 8.82 percent. In China, 50 Internet Service Providers are competing for an Internet user base that increased 1,150 percent in 1996 and 800 percent in 1997, according to the Mosaic Group.[5] Even in the least-developed continent, Africa, the Internet is catching on quickly. The consensus of participants in a 1998 workshop sponsored by the World Bank was that, "spurred by the lower cost of communications and led by the private sector, the use of the Internet is growing rapidly in Africa."[6]

On the supply side, major investments in international Internet connectivity are flooding the marketplace. For example, in March 1998, Level 3—a public company with a $10 billion market value—was launched to build a global fiber-optic communication network based entirely on Internet Protocol (IP) technology, a radical departure from the circuit-switching technology of traditional telecommunications companies. In addition, at least five global satellite networks representing $30 billion in investment and offering fixed broadband services as wireless complements to the terrestrial networks will be operational in the next five years. One such network, Space Way, plans to offer wireless high-speed data and Internet access for between $30 to $40 month, with expected customer equipment, including antennae and PC interface devices, to be priced at or below $1,000 per subscriber. Teledesic, a Bill Gates–backed project undertaken by Boeing Corporation, has the ambition to create an "Internet in the Sky" capable of significantly higher speeds than terrestrial Internets, by linking 840 low-earth-orbit satellites at a cost of $9 billion.

These technology trends point to the increasing availability of a truly global and pervasive information network that can be used for extraordinary supply-chain connectivity. Internet-enabled networks help organizations to attain a much closer alignment with their suppliers. Business-to-business transactions are in fact the most dynamic areas of growth on the World Wide Web.

Major companies have already led the way in creating Internet-enabled supply chains. General Electric (GE) now is linked to its 80,000 suppliers worldwide via an extranet. The company bought more than $1 billion of supplies through the Internet in 1997, a figure GE predicts will rise fivefold by 2000.

In the process of establishing these linkages, GE developed some tools it is now marketing commercially. TPN Register, a joint venture between GE Information Services (GEIS) and the Thomas Register of American Manufacturers, is an Internet-based electronic catalog and ordering system that enables desktop access for buyers to identify suppliers for maintenance and repair orders, spot buys, and unplanned buys. A GEIS companion product, TPNPost, allows buyers to prepare bid packages, select suppliers, and post packages to a secure Web site. It allows suppliers to receive initial bid packages, to prepare and post bids, and to conduct multiround bids online. Hewlett-Packard has claimed that using TPNPost enabled a 50 percent reduction in request-for-quotes processing time while achieving 100 percent data accuracy. GEIS itself claims that TPNPost enables its clients' procurement departments to prepare bids in hours rather than weeks, virtually to eliminate paper and postage costs, to save 10 to 20 percent on material costs, and to slash sourcing cycle times by 50 to 60 percent.

Most major enterprise resources planning vendors are scrambling to integrate Internet-enabled procurement into their products' functionality by the year 2000. For example, SAP's invoicing and transaction systems will link to Web-based procurement systems by 2000; and Oracle plans to release Web-enabled versions of its large-scale relational database products even earlier.

Despite the availability of more open Internet-enabled information-sharing architectures, one hard fact has become clear: Companies are finding that more and more business-critical information now resides outside their organizational control. "We are increasingly dependent on our trading partners of all types (vendors, carriers, logistics service providers, etc.)," explains Peter Stiles, president of Advantage Design, Chicago.[7] "The information about their component of the supply chain exists in their computer systems, not ours."

The ideal supply-chain system, Stiles believes, would allow companies to create a plan, monitor its execution, and analyze the results and feedback to improve actions. Creating such visibility requires that companies obtain 100 percent of the necessary data across the supply chain and not just for isolated business functions. Supply-chain visibility requires being able to monitor the execution of the plan to determine if the plan is being actualized and to detect problems in time to take corrective action. This means analyzing performance-to-plan while the business process is taking place, and being able to analyze historical trends to improve the process over time.

In fact, pioneering companies have been realizing such benefits through integrated information systems for some time. State-of-the-art supply-chain information systems allow companies to track product through the extended supply-chain network, that is, tracking the transit of a product through brokers, ocean carriers, trucking companies, customer warehouses, and so on. This tracking is done on a product or stock keeping unit (SKU) level, not on a shipment level. "This means you can know at any time how many size 8 blue dresses are moving to your distribution center, and exactly where they are in the pipeline," notes John Williford, president of Menlo Logistics, a third-party logistics service provider. "Retail stores now regularly collect product depletion data from barcodes at the checkout counter, and send it back along the supply chain virtually on a real-time basis. This alerts every operating station in the supply chain to the fact that, sooner or later, they will be moving an item that a customer just bought. This phenomenon is rapidly eliminating investment in what was once known as safety stock."

Such global tracking is made possible by the development in the last three or four years of various technologies for tracing volume in each lane, and making informed transportation and logistics decisions. "It tells us what's coming by air and sea, with timed location and status information possible while product is in transit," explained one executive of a third-party logistics firm. "Information is much more specific than in the past. We're getting to the point where we know more about what's in the trailer as well as where that trailer is."

In striving to gain full-spectrum global supply-chain visibility and strategic control over the chain, companies are seeking to create a virtual process across all the functional islands—whether within the trading organization or among trading partners. *Message dialogue* (structured electronic conversations) between functional islands is an emerging concept to integrate the supply chain in a virtual communications process. Then, intelligent messaging allows companies to build an integrated execution monitor that receives messages from all sources, classifies them by event (e.g., production delays, late shipments, backorders, damages), and acts on events, most commonly in the form of notifications to either people or other computer systems. "The goal of intelligent messaging is to deliver decisionable information—information that makes a difference—to the right people as soon as possible so we can accelerate business processes," notes Peter Stiles.[8]

A version of this next-generation decision-support system has already been prototyped by Digital Equipment Corporation. Its Global Supply Chain Model *(GSCM)* has been used to evaluate supply-chain options and plan production and distribution activities. It enabled DEC to lower its cumulative costs by $1 billion and reduce its assets by $400 million while increasing its output by 500 percent.

➤ Holistic Supply-Chain Management Methods

"Too many corporations," says Bruce Westbrook, a consultant with Coopers & Lybrand (now Price Waterhouse, Coopers) in Cleveland, "create well-manicured, operationally efficient departments that have very little connection to other departments within the organization, or to other entities on the outside."[9]

Typically, top management encourages this kind of segmentation and departmentalization because of its practice of viewing order processing, transportation, warehousing, inventory control, packaging, and related support activities as individual cost centers. Few executives take the time to analyze service costs incurred at the customer, product, or even channel level. However, senior executives' ability to manage supply-chain costs and therefore the profitability of a company is dependent on their ability to take a holistic approach to the company's operations. They must be concerned with how products are sourced, manufactured, bought, sold, moved, and merchandised, and ultimately whether customers are satisfied.

To achieve a holistic view, new activity-based costing approaches are important to relate these fragmented facts into meaningful, manageable performance measures. Income statements should reveal the impact of purchasing, materials requirements planning, and production scheduling and control on the cost of goods sold. In addition, it is important to create organizational and process links and seamless information within a corporation among marketing, sales, purchasing, finance, manufacturing, distribution, and transportation, as well as externally to customers, suppliers, carriers and retailers.

➤ Global Third-Party Logistics Providers

Global logistics companies are now acting as systems integrators for major corporate clients, conducting elaborate, highly sequenced "milk runs" to pick up and deliver components and products with a whole host of suppliers and vendors on an international basis. These companies are serving as single-source logistics managers providing load pooling and freight consolidation, air and ocean freight forwarding and local drayage, customs brokerage, and warehousing and distribution. They establish real-time communications between customers, major carriers, and terminals to manage equipment and facilities efficiently and to smooth the peaks and valleys in demand and availability. In other words, they manage the entire global supply chain stretching to the final customers.

For example, a global corporation that produces and distributes personal computers and related products has created a partnership with a third-party logistics provider. This partnership effectively outsources the total global supply chain to the third party, which is responsible for planning and moving all parts, subassembly components, and finished goods between suppliers' facilities, the computer company's production sites, and customers' distribution centers. The computer company reports a high degree of satisfaction with the arrangement, which allows the company to:

➤ Avoid sunk costs in information systems and warehousing capacity.

➤ Gain greater market leverage over ocean, air, and surface transport service providers and receive volume purchasing discounts through aggregating its shipment base with those of the provider's other clients.

➤ Achieve greater flexibility in meeting the needs of customers through access to more diverse channels to the customer.

Such an arrangement would have been unthinkable only a few short years before. The third-party logistics industry has only recently flourished on a global basis, and moved its bases of operation far beyond the United States and Europe to other regions. For example, UPS has formed an alliance with a local third-party logistics firm in India to expand its theater of operations to that subcontinent and to offer its own international corporate clients better logistics management options.

The stature of the global third-party logistics industry will surely grow as it increasingly addresses the supply-chain integration challenges faced by globally expanding corporations from the Organization for Economic Cooperation and Development (OECD) as well as from emerging-market countries. Chapters 4 and 5 discuss outsourcing to third-party providers in greater detail and outline best practices in outsourcing selection and management.

➤ High-Velocity Intermodalism

Intermodal transportation is rapidly becoming the major approach to international cargo transportation, with over 93 million 20-foot equivalent unit containers handled worldwide each year.

Some major companies have gotten quite proficient in managing the complex scheduling and efficient operational handoffs required to exploit new intermodal opportunities. For example, five times a week the Toyota Motor Company's auto assembly plant in Georgetown, Kentucky, receives just-in-time shipments of parts that were loaded onto containers in Japan, shipped as ocean freight across the Pacific, and then switched back to trains on the West Coast for delivery to Georgia. This is merely one intermodal supply flow in Toyota's global network spanning 35 manufacturing plants in 25 countries.

In the United States and Europe, intermodal development is a major strategic priority of government. The recently authorized Intermodal Surface Transportation Act in the United States will authorize billions of dollars over the next few years to help regions and states improve connections between modes as a catalyst for economic growth. We can anticipate more intensive portfolio-management approaches toward intermodal assets. Ports, air cargo resources, feeder road and rail systems, and professional services support resources increasingly will be managed as integrated interconnected systems from a strategic investment and operational deployment/maintenance perspective. These approaches will certainly help support continued efficiency of global supply chains.

➤ Government Trade Facilitation Systems

New trade facilitation systems implemented by national governments have also supported the globalization of supply chains. Singapore is a vanguard example of this trend. Its trade-permitting process allows traders to fill out only a single electronic form. This form can be transmitted to the Trade Development Board's mainframe computer on a 24-hour basis. The mainframe then routes it electronically to 18 different agencies involved in trade permitting. Approvals are sent to a trader's electronic mailbox within 15 minutes. Estimated savings to traders from reduced paperwork have been $1 billion a year.

Mexico is another important example of these new, computer-based trading systems. Prior to massive reengineering, the trading and customs system in Mexico was highly centralized under the Directorate General of Customs, and traders faced long delays in the processing and clearing of merchandise. Computerization reduced the steps in the customs process from 12 to four, resulting in substantial process time reductions. By 1990, all major customs sites were electronically networked in a shared system. The results have been dramatic. For example, at Nuevo Laredo, the main trucking entry point from the United States, the number of operations handled daily went from 800 to 1200, and the normal processing time per transaction was sliced from three days to 20 minutes. Based on these results, the improvements represent an estimated annualized savings of more than U.S. $2 billion.

The U.S. Customs Service also is reengineering to facilitate trade in the twenty-first century. It has launched a reorganization to reduce headquarters staffing by about 600 positions (about one-third); reduce management layers from four to three by eliminating seven regions and 42 districts and replacing them with 20 management centers; redirecting people from headquarter, region, and district offices into operational field positions to enhance responsiveness to customers; and invest in information technology and the Customers Automated Commercial System (ACS). Marian Duntley, director, import services for DHL Worldwide Express, elaborated on the benefits of this new approach:

> *The most exciting thing with [Customs'] new system is remote filing, where we will be able to funnel all of that information that comes from overseas into a DHL processing center instead of having to process all of that data in different sites. Currently, we have six different sites where we process entry data. We'll be able to consolidate all of those into one or two processing centers*

and communicate directly with Customs on the entry process side—all the while utilizing a number of import gateways for the actual physical movement of the freight.

■ MANAGEMENT BEST PRACTICES ARE EVOLVING

The combined effects of the above trends will be profound, and will surely accelerate the growth of logistics/supply-chain management as the organizational hub of the global extended enterprise. Based on these trends, we believe that managing the extended enterprise will increasingly focus on these three domains of best practice:

➤ *Physical network management,* which seeks to exert strategic control over the physical distribution chain to the customer. It allows new efficiencies in the movement of goods and services both inside the enterprise and between the enterprise and its distribution and supply partners.

➤ *Information and knowledge network management,* which seeks to exert strategic control over business-to-business and business-to-consumer transactions conducted via private value-added networks or the Internet. This domain aggressively uses dynamic knowledge management systems to better visualize supply chain flows, capture organizationwide learning about operations, and improve performance.

➤ *Computer-based infrastructure management,* which seeks to acquire and capitalize on a more efficient and responsive regional, national, and international supply-chain support infrastructure to raise corporate total factor productivity. This domain includes highly automated government customs/cargo clearance systems and national EDI systems; hub/spoke intermodal transportation systems with more seamless handoffs between air, sea, and overland shipping modes; dispatch/routing/vehicle and traffic management systems; and shared assets such as public bonded warehouses or telecommunications/online network resources.

Companies that can manage these practices and domains in an integrated and effective way will continue to reap large benefits. Although forecasting the impacts of these practices over the next decade is a high-risk activity, we have nevertheless attempted a thought exercise with the objective of formulating a new chronology of supply-chain management that incorporates past, present, and future development phases into a continuum. Figure 1.2, beginning on page 26, depicts the evolution of supply-chain management best practices through the year 2010 to the fully extended enterprise model.

■ IMPROVING YOUR COMPANY'S SUPPLY-CHAIN COMPETENCE

To create and manage an extended enterprise for competitive advantage, senior management must begin by addressing the challenges of segmenting and focusing the supplier base and establishing strategic partnerships. Key alliances include those with core materials and components suppliers, transportation suppliers, warehousing and distribution center service providers, and third-party logistics companies, who provide supply-chain system modeling and optimization strategies and management assistance packages to implement improvements. These relationships will form the bloodlines and oxygen flow of the extended enterprise.

	1990 Higher-Level Corporate Model	2000 Extended Enterprise Model	2010 Fully Extended Enterprise Model
Supply-chain strategic orientation	Management focus on integrated physical distribution and customer service sides of supply chain.	Management focus on building extended transactions/communications platforms to integrate global physical, service, and information flows between key value chain actors.	Management focus on exploiting the highly intelligent IT-enabled global value chain, with emphasis on continuous exchange of not only data sets but also dynamic knowledge flows about market events and customer drivers.
	Interest in mapping and costing supply-chain network activities to exert real strategic control over the extended enterprise for the first time.	Interest in optimizing physical/electronic value chains based on cost/benefit analyses of total costs of asset ownership on each step of the value chain and outsourcing.	Interest in the direct substitution of information for physical assets and the deployment of massive global bandwidth to create new global supply-chain capabilities.
Leadership structure	Higher-level executive (chief logistics officer) seeks to compress cycle times to customer and provide efficient cross-functional operational handoffs.	VP for the "All Channels Supply Chain" manages internal/external assets and physical/informational transactions as one seamless web.	Chief executive officer leads formalization of knowledge capture/management systems across the extended supply chain.
			(continues)

Figure 1.2 The projected evolution of supply chain management best practices.

	1990 Higher-Level Corporate Model	2000 Extended Enterprise Model	2010 Fully Extended Enterprise Model
	Director of electronic commerce is creating information infrastructure for the extended enterprise and is emerging as a key corporate opinion maker in supply-chain management.	Director of logistics (Physical Channels) and director of E-Commerce (Electronic Channels) report to VP of an "All-Channels Supply Chain."	The Supply-Chain Change Group acts as the hub of knowledge to intelligently capture, classify, analyze, summarize, and route knowledge to its most appropriate users.
	Internal units aggregate purchasing, shipment, and information system requirements to lower transaction costs and gain leverage over vendors.	An "All Channels Supply-Chain Change Group" composed of people drawn from across the extended enterprise, from distributors/suppliers/carriers.	Management of multichannel global customer order interfaces: e-commerce-enabled Web sites/phone order systems and wholesale/retail outlets.
Nature of relationships	Shift to core long-range strategic alliances with carriers, suppliers, and distributors; emphasis is on operational cost reduction.	Shift to wider sourcing of services and products; emphasis is on reliability and reduction of volatility to deliver better customer service in a globalizing marketplace.	Shift to optimizing global supply chains; emphasis is on systematic evaluation of the universe of global sourcing options for products and services at every step of the supply chain.

Figure 1.2 Continued

	1990 Higher-Level Corporate Model	2000 Extended Enterprise Model	2010 Fully Extended Enterprise Model
	Core distributors/suppliers/ carriers moving to real-time operations connectivity over private corporate networks or over emerging Internet-based networks.	Core distributors/suppliers/ carriers moving to real-time connectivity for collaborative forecasting and planning; shift to knowledge management.	Core distributors/suppliers/ carriers moving to high-level synchronization of knowledge, actions, and schedules across globally distributed supply chains.
	Extranet data backbone enables "real-time windows" on internal operations to open to core suppliers and distributors.	First use of global online bidding/sourcing systems on the Internet for both core suppliers as well as spot suppliers to slash order cycle time.	Real-time dynamic supply-chain-wide coordination in response to external events. The realization of the IT-enabled supply chain.
Priority technology applications	Intelligent agents and automated "decision tools" utilize incoming data flows to evaluate inventory levels across the value chain and act to optimize held versus in-transit inventory.	Wholesale shift to the Internet. Major integration efforts aimed at using open Internet front ends and secure EDI back-ends in corporate e-commerce networks, particularly in the order management/customer service area.	Faster switching times and greater multimedia capacity of the Internet enable faster flow-through times in supply-chain pipelines, greater velocity of assets and transactions.

Figure 1.2 Continued

1990 Higher-Level Corporate Model	2000 Extended Enterprise Model	2010 Fully Extended Enterprise Model
Attempt to make supply-chain network modeling software more dynamic, less reliant on batched, slow information transfers.	Electronic messaging enables real-time use of data in supply-chain network modeling.	More extensive and systematic fusing of data and information into "true" supply-chain knowledge. Increased capability to launch real-time optimizing actions across the supply chain.

Figure 1.2 Continued

Senior management must also focus attention on aggregating demand across all purchasing units into corporatewide buys, gaining marketplace leverage, centralizing negotiations with the universe of core materials suppliers and service providers, and extracting greater compliance with corporate supply-chain price, quality, and order/delivery cycle requirements. *This is the beginning of the extended enterprise.* Through these early alliances, companies learn how to cultivate relationships across the supply chain, exchange transaction data, and leap forward into valuable collaborative planning/forecasting across the chain.

The supply-chain management practices that this book elaborates can help companies develop the capabilities they will need to survive and prosper in the twenty-first century. Providing an overview of potential supply-chain improvements, Chapter 2 describes the best practices that have helped today's most successful extended enterprises achieve competitive superiority.

Chapter

Logistics Best Practices

Arthur Andersen Consulting defines best practices as the optimum ways to perform a business process. Because leading organizations have used these approaches to achieve top performance, best practices serve as goals for other companies striving to improve performance and better satisfy stakeholder interests. The first challenge for leaders and managers is identifying which best practices are most appropriate to use in their organization.

In his best-selling book, *Competitive Advantage: Creating and Sustaining Superior Performance,*[1] Michael Porter identified three generic strategies that companies can adopt to achieve competitive advantage in their industries. They can:

1. Become cost leaders; that is, produce goods or services at lower cost than their competitors.

2. Differentiate their products or services in a way that will induce customers to pay a premium for the company offerings.

3. Focus on an industry segment and cater to that segment in a more effective way than the competition.

Adopting logistics/supply-chain best practices can enhance success with any of these strategies. But are the same best practices used by an enterprise pursuing a differentiation strategy also appropriate for a company following a cost leadership focus? Should the upscale department store Bloomingdale's, for example, use the same logistics strategy as mass merchant Wal-Mart? The answer at the operational level, is, of course, no, or at least not necessarily.

Operational best practices vary widely among industries and among firms within industries, depending upon generic strategies and other factors. An inventory policy with a 99 percent fill rate from stock may be appropriate for Wal-Mart but entirely inappropriate for Bloomingdale's, with its high-end, multisized and-styled stockkeeping units. However, at the strategic level, best practices that work for Wal-Mart will likely also work for Bloomingdale's. For instance, while the operational benchmark of achieving a 99 percent fill rate may not be appropriate for both firms, the strategy of setting fill rate objectives and then benchmarking actual performance against these objectives is entirely appropriate for both firms.

This chapter describes strategic-level best practices in logistics and supply-chain management that have helped many organizations improve their performance. The practices cited come from extensive research the authors conducted for the U.S. Department of Energy. This in-depth look at more than two dozen companies' logistics/supply-chain management strategies found that high-performing firms, almost uniformly, follow certain procedures and organizational principles. These best practices include:

➤ Recognizing logistics and supply-chain management as a strategically important set of activities, and developing a mission statement that defines their roles, goals, and vision.

➤ Integrating logistics activities into one department or developing procedures to coordinate logistics activities across the supply chain for better performance.

➤ Centralizing supply-chain management at the corporate level.

➤ Creating a logistics/supply-chain leader, often called a *chief logistics officer,* to allocate resources among supply-chain functions, to optimize trade-offs between functions, and to act as an interface between logistics and the other functional areas within a firm, as well as between the firm and other players in the supply chain.

➤ Developing a clear, transparent set of practices to finance supply-chain management.

➤ Using performance metrics extensively and systematically to measure the performance of logistics activities.

This chapter discusses each of these practices in more detail, explaining necessary actions and potential benefits as well as providing examples of companies that have adopted the approaches successfully.

■ RECOGNIZING THE IMPORTANCE OF LOGISTICS AND SUPPLY-CHAIN MANAGEMENT AND DEVELOPING A MISSION STATEMENT

All companies typically perform a number of activities that can be classified under the terms *logistics* or *supply-chain management.* These activities include all those related to the movement and flow of materials and products, as well as the ancillary flow of information and cash. Coyle, Bardi, and Langley[2] list the following activities under logistics: traffic and transportation, warehousing and storage, industrial

packaging, materials handling, inventory control, order fulfillment, demand forecasting, production planning, purchasing, customer service levels, plant and warehouse site
location, returned-goods handling, parts and service support, and salvage and scrap disposal. Best practices organizations recognize that these activities are part of logistics and
view them not as isolated technical functions but as a strategically important, related set of activities that can create
competitive advantage.

To a large degree, best practices logistics organizations
have emerged because of a unifying and encompassing
vision of logistics. In fact, having a strategic orientation, as
reflected by having the logistics/supply-chain mission as an
integral component of an overall organizational mission, is
the initial step in becoming a best practices organization. In
this view, the primary mission of the logistics department
should be to support corporate goals and strategies in a company's mission statement, with logistics providing a means
to increase quality, achieve customer focus, and improve
efficiencies. For example, if the primary goal of a corporation is to be the industry cost leader, the logistics department needs to develop a mission statement that reflects this
corporate priority.

■ INTEGRATING LOGISTICS ACTIVITIES INTO ONE DEPARTMENT AND COORDINATING LOGISTICS ACTIVITIES ACROSS THE SUPPLY CHAIN

In most companies, the logistics activities listed above are
divided among a number of departments, including purchasing, operations, and marketing. However, best practices
firms typically integrate the operations of these functions,
either formally within a "logistics" department, or less formally, such as through regular interdepartmental managerial meetings, project teams, or shared-reward systems. By

integrating logistics functions, firms can foster synergy within the organization and avoid setting up conflicting goals between departments and managers. For example, by integrating the purchasing department with the traffic or transportation function, a firm will be less likely to have empty trucks arriving at or leaving processing facilities. Traffic managers, who typically control outbound transportation, will be aware of incoming loads and will be in a better position to make use of backhaul possibilities. Likewise, purchasing managers will be less likely to pursue goals in direct conflict with those of warehouse and inventory managers, such as using forward buys to achieve quantity discounts when inventory managers are concerned about clogging warehouses.

Two company examples illustrate the benefits of coordinating logistics functions across a firm. Fellowes Manufacturing realized significant reductions in both cycle time and costs through companywide logistics coordination and reduced its distribution network to two facilities. Lever Brothers went a step further and took an "interfunctional management approach" that interconnected logistics functions with other functions in the organization. This strategy has enabled Lever Brothers' logistics considerations to be incorporated into tactical operations across different functional areas of the organization. In addition, best practices organizations see logistics as the glue that holds together customers, suppliers, transportation carriers, and all other firms in their extended enterprises. Indeed, logistics can be viewed as a core managerial function for firms attempting to manage extended enterprises or to integrate the operations of supply-chain members. One example of the key roles played by the logistics department in supply-chain management is the implementation of supply-chain partnerships with vendors. In some partnerships, suppliers and organizational customers link their information systems so vendors are aware of the inventory levels of their products at customer locations on a real-time basis. This knowledge allows vendors to time production runs and set delivery schedules more precisely. A well-run vendor-managed inventory system reduces inventory costs within the supply chain and enhances the service levels both the vendor and the client customer are able to provide. The vendor can reduce its cycle time, while the customer's inventory fill rate increases.

Implementing a well-functioning vendor-managed inventory system also requires synchronizing logistics functions along the rest of the supply chain (including carriers), as well as cooperation and information-sharing among departments within each organization. This coordination minimizes the transaction costs between vendor and customer organizations and enables vendor investment in dedicated or relation-specific assets, which can lower costs, improve quality, and speed product development.

Although coordination and supply-chain partnerships with vendors have economic benefits, some researchers have found that these relationships are costly to establish and maintain, and may reduce a customer's ability to switch away from inefficient suppliers. In fact, firms in the automotive industry have successfully taken opposite approaches. Toyota, for example, has developed long-term partnerships with suppliers that are given implicit guarantees on future business. In return, suppliers make specific investments to enhance their productivity in the Toyota relationship. General Motors, on the other hand, has historically generated cost savings by fostering vigorous supplier competition and constantly renegotiating contracts. Although critics argue that the long-term negative effects of this strategy are yet to be felt, GM has saved from $3 billion to $4 billion as a result of these tough supplier management practices.

Of course, the key question facing logistics managers is *which model of supplier management is superior?* Firms should think more strategically about supplier management and perhaps should not have a one-size-fits-all strategy. Instead they should analyze each supplier strategically to determine the extent to which the supplier's product contributes to the core competence and competitive advantage of the buying firm.

To this end, we believe that strategic partnerships should be fostered with suppliers that provide inputs of high value and play an important role in differentiating the buyer's final product. The buyer should maintain high levels of communication with these suppliers, provide managerial assistance, exchange personnel, make relation-specific investments, and make every effort to ensure that these suppliers have world-class capabilities.

On the other hand, relationships with commodity-based suppliers providing standardized inputs do not contribute to the competitive advantage of the buyer's final product. These relationships will be characterized by less-frequent communication, less assistance, fewer relation-specific investments, and frequent price benchmarking.

■ CENTRALIZING SUPPLY-CHAIN MANAGEMENT AT THE CORPORATE LEVEL

It has been traditional for organizations to view logistics as an operational function, responsible for activities such as warehousing, materials management, and transportation. As an operational function, logistics control has been located at operational levels of organizations—at the strategic business unit (SBU) level, at the plant level, or at the distribution center level. However, the integrated logistics/supply-chain approach described above is inconsistent with an organizational structure that has logistics managed and controlled at lower levels of an organization. For example, it is not possible to achieve maximal cost savings across an organization if individual plants or strategic business units are allowed to select carriers without regard for the choices of other units in an organization. Likewise, organizationwide customer service standards and organizationwide risk-management programs for warehousing or transporting hazardous materials cannot be established without central managerial control over logistics.

Of course, not all activities need to be centralized in all companies. Best practices companies use the following guidelines in deciding what aspects of their logistics systems to centralize:

> Centralize the management and control of those logistics activities that allow the firm to achieve operational efficiencies or other synergies through a centralized approach.

> Decentralize only those logistics activities that do not offer organizationwide synergies.

Figure 2.1 lists logistics activities that are either centralized or left decentralized in best practices firms.

Many benefits can be achieved by centralizing the management and control of logistics functions across an organization. A number of these benefits are discussed below.

Centrally Located	Decentralized
Strategic Planning	Materials Handling
Master Scheduling	Inventory Management
Distribution Planning	Warehousing Operations
Purchasing	Receiving and Staging
Carrier Qualification	Private Fleet Management
Freight Payments	Returns
Order Processing	
Rate Negotiations	
Risk Management	
Information Technology Management	

Figure 2.1 Location of functions and responsibilities.

Benefit 1: Full Realization of Economies of Scale in Purchasing Both Raw Materials and Transportation Services

A centralized purchasing department not only allows firms to group purchases to obtain the largest quantity discounts, but it can also lead to the standardization of materials, thereby reducing stockkeeping units and inventory carrying costs. Standardized purchasing through a central purchasing department can also better accommodate transshipments between stocking points, since the various stockkeeping locations are more likely to be holding the same materials or products.

Centralized partnerships between shippers and carriers have played a critical role in improving productivity and performance in transportation and distribution. Motor carriers like Matlack and Bee Line have forged strong partnerships with their shippers, Air Products and Monsanto, respectively, in areas of compliance and safety to create synergies that have benefited both parties. Other partnerships focus on cost containment and improved performance through shared information and an increased understanding of both partners' needs. Shippers and carriers like Pierdot Chemical and Chemical Leaman, and Goodyear Tire and Yellow Freight have established long-term partnerships and, as a result, both parties have realized increased flexibility, more accurate resource forecasting, bipartisan scheduling, and more reliable performance.

Critics of centralized purchasing departments often point out that these units tend to rely less on local suppliers. Transportation costs may increase, these same critics charge, as a result of buying centrally from long-distance suppliers. In response to the first criticism, although centralized purchasing may reduce reliance on some local suppliers, it also creates greater opportunities for (formerly) local suppliers to obtain wider supply mandates. Therefore, centralized purchasing may turn a small, local supplier into a much larger source of supply for the firm. As for the second criticism, centralized purchasing departments must, of course, make decisions based on total landed costs. To the extent that transportation costs are high for particular products or materials, relative to purchase and holding costs, these purchases will tend to be made locally. A central purchasing department does not preclude local purchasing. It serves to rationalize purchasing decisions with local pur-

FRITO-LAY: CENTRALIZED SUPPLY CHAIN PLANNING IN ACTION

As detailed in a Harvard Business School case study, Frito-Lay, the largest manufacturer of salty snacks in the United States, operates numerous plants across the United States to produce the majority of its products. Except for a few minor specialty items, which are purchased from outside suppliers, core and specialty products alike are produced by Frito-Lay. Each plant, however, does not handle shipments of final products autonomously.

Frito-Lay has a centralized Product-Supply Group in charge of planning and scheduling shipments of diverse mixes of final products from each plant to cover Frito-Lay's markets across the United States. The Product-Supply Group optimizes the firm's operation by assigning product shipments and market coverage to the manufacturing plants that can supply Frito-Lay's points of consolidation and sale at the lowest distribution costs. Frito-Lay officials call this system "Darwinian," because efficient plants survive by getting larger service areas, and plants compete with one another to increase their market coverage.

During its first year of existence, the Product-Supply Group made market-area reassignments that resulted in savings of more than $10 million. Subsequent years typically have seen 20 market-area changes moving a total of 10 million pounds of products from one plant to another, with a net annual savings to the company of $1.5 million.

chases made when they are cost effective and with centralized purchases made when they are cost effective.

Centralized purchasing departments are becoming
increasingly easier to implement with the use of the Internet and modern modes of communication. Best practices
companies, such as General Electric, have already realized
that the World Wide Web allows qualified companies from
around the world to bid easily on purchase orders by check-
ing requests for quotes and proposals and submitting bids
over the Internet.

Benefit 2: One Set of Rules and Procedures that Can Be Enforced at the Headquarters Level

A second advantage of centralized logistics management is
that it allows firms to establish a single set of rules and procedures enforced on a corporatewide basis. This does not
imply that actual standards must be uniform across the
organization, but only that the methods used to arrive at the
standards should be uniform or centrally controlled. For
example, a company with several distribution centers
around the country or the world may set different fill rates
for each of the distribution centers. However, corporatewide
rules and procedures, based on the company's mission and
strategy, should guide the establishment of the fill rates.
Therefore, a 90 percent fill rate may be acceptable at a distribution center with overnight transshipment possibilities
from a second center, whereas a geographically isolated center may require a 98 percent fill rate.

Risk management and safety offer another example of
the value of centralized rule-making. For example, multina-
tional firms engaged in the transportation of hazardous
materials must be aware of myriad local, state, and national
rules and regulations. It would be inviting, therefore, for
these firms to delegate the enforcement of these ordinances
to field units, which may be thought to have the best knowl-

edge of the local ordinances. However, field unit personnel may not be aware of companywide ramifications that can result from their oversight of hazardous materials, or lack thereof. A hazardous materials spill in a developing country, causing death or pollution of the environment, may, courtesy of CNN and other news organizations, result in negative publicity all over the world. Even if the developing country lacks tight environmental rules or enforcement procedures, it is probably not in the company's best interests to adopt lax risk management procedures. Even if it were, the decision should be made at the corporate level, not the local level.

Union Carbide, a leading producer of plastics and chemicals, learned this lesson the hard way. After its accident in its plant in Bopahl, India in 1984, it assembled a headquarters triad composed of a *risk/regulatory compliance officer,* an *operating officer* (with oversight of physical facilities), and a *commercial officer* (with oversight of all outsourcing and carrier policies). This group was placed in charge of the risk management and policy program for the entire corporation. The triad was given responsibility for translating strategic business unit requirements and selecting outside suppliers of services and materials; auditing outside carriers against existing policies and procedures and taking corrective actions against violators; directing emergency response programs; acting as an agent for the company in regulatory affairs and compliance; and scheduling risk management audits that cover purchasing, warehousing, material handling, and transportation functions throughout the firm's value chain.

Benefit 3: A System of Coordinated Information Flows

Central management and control of information technology within an organization can minimize information system incompatibilities—one of the greatest barriers to achieving operational efficiencies. In some cases, information system incompatibility or diversity results from organizational acquisitions or mergers, with each organization bringing its own system into the larger firm. However, even single organizations that lack central control and oversight over information technology may wind up with incompatible systems.

Centralized control offers a variety of benefits. Companies such as Baxter Health Care have been able to reduce their costs and improve their response rates by designing their logistic work flows and processes through centralized electronic data interchange (EDI) systems. Centralization for system compatibility also makes it easier to conduct internal benchmarking, develop centralized purchasing capabilities, facilitate and coordinate transshipments, or engage in other activities that require close coordination.

Information systems created the opportunity for companies like Sun Chemical to centralize the coordination and control of its logistics operations while significantly reducing staff. The flow of electronic information to and from Sun's 187 field locations has enabled a traffic staff of only four people to monitor and track nearly 650 million tons of less-than-truckload freight every year. Electronic data flow and management have also allowed Bee Line to track down its hazardous material shipments by satellite in real-time, increasing the flow of critical information needed to respond in case of an accident. Software systems like those available from LogicNet, ProfitMax, and Transportation Concepts and Services have increased the awareness of present and future logistics activities among users. Indeed, these computer packages have proven to be a powerful instrument in planning, scheduling, monitoring, and tracking flow performance and status of shipments.

Technology has spurred improvements in many other areas as well. Saia Freight and Country Skillet worked together using integrated designs and new cooling and control technologies to create a customized packaging system.

The new system, called Pallet Reefer, incorporates customer requirements and transportation capabilities into a new generation of logistics packaging products. Bee Line uses on-board text computers to keep drivers continuously informed of changes in road and traffic conditions, congestion patterns, and other situational factors affecting performance.

In summary, centralized control over logistics allows for the creation of unified, integrated information systems that can help companies achieve operational efficiencies.

■ CREATING A CHIEF LOGISTICS OFFICER

If an organization is to have a centrally controlled logistics department, it must also have a corporate-level logistics leader. This is the role played by chief logistics officers (CLOs), or similarly titled individuals, in best practice organizations. CLOs have a global view of logistics activities and the decision-making authority to set priorities for logistics activities and coordinate with other parts of the organization. As indicated later in this book, the CLO position is vital to centralized and/or integrated logistics management, even (perhaps especially) if an organization has outsourced its entire supply chain. In this situation, the CLO takes on the critical role of in-house management of contract services. Other key roles of a CLO in a best practices firm include:

> ➤ *Reconciling trade-offs and conflicts between logistics and other functions.* For example, purchasing departments often prefer to order in bulk to realize the largest discounts from suppliers. Transportation managers may prefer bulk purchases as well, in order to obtain truckload discounts on inbound loads. Inventory managers, on the other hand, usually prefer smaller, more frequent

purchase orders to reduce inventory on hand. Which department gets its way? A CLO can provide the standards and procedures for reconciling these conflicts in the best interests of the firm.

➤ *Determining how to allocate the capital budget for logistics among the logistics functions and activities.* A CLO, with a broad view of logistics within an organization, is in the best position to determine which warehouse needs to be expanded, what trucks need to be purchased, and which conveyor system needs to be installed.

➤ *Serving as an interface between logistics and other functions within the organization and between the organization and other supply chain members.* Just as conflicts and trade-offs need to be reconciled within the logistics department, they also need to be reconciled between departments and between members of the supply chain. The CLO negotiates on behalf of the logistics department within the firm and on behalf of the firm within the supply chain.

➤ *Managing internal and external logistics benchmarking activities.* Benchmarking involves establishing metrics, collecting data to measure the metrics, computing the metrics, and comparing metrics among units in the organization (internal benchmarking) and between the organization and other firms (external benchmarking).

➤ *Managing outsourcing activities.* As noted above, contracting logistics functions to third parties does not relieve a firm of the responsibility for managing logistics activities. The CLO can manage the selection process of third-party contractors, be the point person in the negotiation of contracts, set and evaluate performance metrics used to assess their performance, conduct regular meetings to discuss performance, and determine whether contracts should be renewed. Chapter 5 has more details on logistics outsourcing and related management challenges.

TAPPING LOGISTICS FOR COMPETITIVE ADVANTAGE

Companies that adopt the logistics best practices outlined in this chapter have one thing in common—they view logistics as an engine for competitive advantage, not as merely a technical function. As a result, they are able to reap huge benefits from managing logistics from this strategic position. The experiences of companies like Nynex and the Polaroid Corporation illustrate the value of this evolution in logistics' stature from a mere function to a generator of competitive advantage.

At Polaroid, the need to improve customer satisfaction levels prompted a full-fledged reengineering process to integrate the firm's functional silos and unite logistics and customer service in a continuous process. As part of this process, Polaroid planners critically examined how well the company fulfilled its customers' needs. This study revealed that the company's vertically focused organization structure impeded Polaroid's ability to serve its customers effectively. To improve performance, therefore, the company linked previously separate functions such as order entry, accounting, and customer service into a seamless, integrated process-platform controlled by corporate-level logistics and marketing executives.

Nynex Corporation, a major regional U.S. telecommunications company now owned by Bell Atlantic, undertook a major overhaul of its supply-chain network to effect significant savings and operational improvements. Specifically, Nynex closed two of its three warehouses, and computerized the remaining one for synchronized materials management. This consolidation and systems upgrade slashed inventory of spare parts, materials, and tools for field technicians from $50 million to $23 million over a 10-year period. As part of this same effort, Nynex slashed the number of different items it purchased from 8,000 to 3,800, and revamped customer order processing by incorporating information technology equipment such as barcode scanners and EDI systems. The reengineering project paid for itself the first year, allowing Nynex to save several million dollars a year. From the outset, the project received top management support. In fact, senior executives viewed the changes as a vital opportunity to gain competitive advantage in the deregulated U.S. telecommunications industry.

■ DEVELOPING A CLEAR, TRANSPARENT SET OF PRACTICES TO FINANCE CENTRALIZED LOGISTICS MANAGEMENT

One of the major impediments to the creation of centralized logistics groups is that these groups are often viewed as overhead. Since revenues are generated at the SBU level, no funds may be allocated for centralized logistics management. Some firms handle the financing of a centralized logistics group through direct budget allocations. However, the question often arises whether the firm is "getting its money's worth" from the group. Other companies organize centralized logistics groups as cost centers, with the group measured on the basis of cost savings. However, cost savings by the group are difficult to assess since the strategic business units will realize most of these savings, which may be difficult to attribute to the centralized logistics group. Still other firms organize their centralized logistics groups as profit centers. The profit center organization is also difficult to implement since revenue payments by the SBUs to the centralized unit may be based on internal transfer prices, rather than on market prices.

In our work, we did not determine one best method for structuring the financing of centralized logistics groups. However, certain practices were characteristic of best practice organizations. They include the following:

➤ *Keeping the financing of logistics units simple and clearly understood by the strategic business units.* Cost and revenue transfers are made transparent to all concerned parties.

➤ *Ensuring that centralized logistics units operate efficiently, by benchmarking these units against those of external organizations and by allowing SBUs, when feasible, to obtain logistics services from outside the organization if they can obtain better values.* For example, logistics personnel at the plant or division level can, at times, obtain transportation rates below those negotiated by the central logistics unit. When this occurs, the divisions are allowed to use the less-expensive carriers as long as this strategy does not have a negative impact on the national rate structure—and as long as the new carrier meets the corporatewide carrier qualifications.

➤ *Developing chargeback procedures whereby the cost of the central logistics unit is charged back to the SBUs on the basis of use.* The SBUs monitor the activities of the central units so that they can verify their assessed portion of the operating costs.

■ USING PERFORMANCE METRICS EXTENSIVELY AND SYSTEMATICALLY

In best practices organizations, performance metrics are an essential management tool for logistics (as well as other functional areas). Performance metrics involve adapting statistical process control theory to the measurement of logistics performance. Companies use performance metrics to benchmark cost, revenue, and customer service performance between departments; within a department over a period of time; and externally against organizations both inside and outside the firm's primary industry. For example, companies from a variety of industries benchmark their service levels against catalogue merchant L.L. Bean, which is known for world-class customer service. Best practices firms have been called "compulsive performance measurers" in that they use performance metrics to monitor and compare performance continuously at the organization, SBU, and department levels. In our surveys of best practices organizations, we found that these organizations use extensive, regular, and systematic performance measurements to improve performance. They also operate according to the philosophy, "Measure what you manage, and manage what you measure."

Major performance metrics in logistics management fall into a number of categories. In general, performance metrics can be used to assess the costs of operations, the revenues generated from operations, the productivity of logistics employees or logistics assets, and the levels of customer service provided by logistics units. Broad performance metric categories and sample metrics within each category would, therefore, include the following:

➤ General logistics cost metrics, including measures of warehousing cost or transportation cost that firms use to benchmark against similar companies, benchmark the organization over time against itself, and benchmark departments against each other.

➤ Asset management metrics, including measures such as inventory turnover or fleet assets per shipment, that best practices companies use to determine how well they are utilizing scarce resources.

➤ Service metrics, such as fill rate, cycle time, or on-time delivery rate, used to assess the customer service performance of the organization.

➤ Productivity metrics, such as shipments per employee or logistics cost per employee, which help determine problem areas within an organization or assess the performance of an organization against competitors.

It is important to note that the metrics, themselves, do not provide solutions to problems facing organizations. Metrics are diagnostic tools that can help locate potential problem areas and trigger further investigation. For example, poor on-time performance for outbound deliveries may be due to software problems in a vehicle routing system or to some other internal problem, but may also be due to unavoidable bad weather. In any case, a dip in a performance metric should trigger an investigation to find the actual cause of the problem and develop an appropriate solution.

Metric-driven programs for performance improvements have been very effective in improving the execution of logistics functions in many companies. For example, they have allowed companies like Subaru (North America) to transform its logistics functions into a source of competitive advantage. For years, parts distribution at Subaru had been plagued with problems, delays, and poor quality. As the industry moved to a more competitive and customer-driven orientation, Subaru realized that its parts supply process desperately needed improvement. Subaru's vice president of logistics implemented a broad-based quality improvement process based on systematic performance metrics and regular reviews.

Subaru developed a performance metrics scorecard based on a 100-point system in nine categories, to measure almost all aspects of its supply-chain process. Each activity is weighted and scored on a number of different criteria. Each month, the performance metrics are tabulated and the results presented for discussion among appropriate activity managers. The final tally is used as a basis for targeting quality improvement programs. The result has been dramatic improvements in quality, timeliness, and productivity.

■ ADOPTING BEST PRACTICES: THE CHALLENGES OF CHANGE

Adopting the approaches discussed in this chapter can bring many benefits to company performance and thus to stakeholders. However, the logistics best practices our research identified were often very different from the traditional practices many companies continue to follow. Developing a world-class logistics operation that provides competitive advantage and supports corporate goals may require radical rethinking and redesign of logistics activities, which in turn requires commitment, resources, and time to implement. It is also likely to accompany or provoke change in other activities or other parts of the company—and possibly in the organization as a whole. For example, an integrated, centrally managed supply chain could not operate as effectively in a functionally organized firm.

In addition, adopting logistics best practices cannot be done in isolation. It will involve at a minimum the support of top leadership and managers of related units and the help of nonlogistics experts, such as financial specialists, those skilled in developing performance metrics, and those with experience in managing change, including the human resources effects of new approaches and norms.

As a result, the process of change itself helps to link the logistics function more directly and routinely to other parts of the company. Such integration is vital for a strategically focused approach to succeed.

Chapter 3

Best Practices Companies in Action

As explained in Chapters 1 and 2, the logistics field has undergone a number of changes as a result of technological and competitive forces. Although research into modern logistics dates back to the beginning of the twentieth century, many companies, in both service and manufacturing industries, only recognized logistics as a separate functional entity during the 1960s. Before then, logistics was considered a subfunctional entity buried within marketing or manufacturing departments.

Once logistics was identified as a separate functional division in the firm, companies started gradually to learn more about the managerial processes involved in this newly discovered field. Since the early 1970s, many of those companies began adjusting their logistics processes and optimizing their logistics infrastructures. Over the last three decades, these firms have adopted multiple techniques in order to improve their supply-chain performance. However, only those enterprises that have been able to successfully plan, organize, operate, monitor, and control those changes realized the highest performance improvements.[1]

There are remarkable differences between leading-edge logistics management practices today and what were con-

sidered leading-edge logistics management practices 20 or
30 years ago. Companies have shifted their logistics orientation from within their warehouses and manufacturing
plants to their customers. Companies have also redesigned
their organizational structures, along with their logistics
functional systems, to reduce the financial resources committed to physical assets and human resources. In addition, companies have found that by redesigning their
logistics infrastructures they are better able to centrally
manage and synchronize their flows of materials, products,
and information and obtain economies of scale and
economies of conjunction. Furthermore, firms have closer
informational links with suppliers of parts and raw materials that have allowed them to substitute information for
inventory and thereby reduce total stock levels dramati-
cally. Finally, companies have become aware that third-
party logistics providers with economies of scale, and
dedicated knowledge and assets, can be more effective at
performing logistics functions than can the companies
themselves, especially when such functions are outside
their core competencies.

This chapter examines the experiences of companies
that have successfully incorporated the best practices outlined in Chapter 2 into their logistics operations. Although
no single company exemplifies all the leading-edge logistics
practices, these case study companies have succeeded in
adopting some of the practices most appropriate to their
competitive situations. Our analysis of these enterprises is
based on information obtained in the University of Maryland Supply Chain Management Center study mentioned
earlier, and conducted over the course of several years for
the U.S. Department of Energy. The ensuing discussion
aims to provide practical details about the significant logis-
tics/supply-chain management practices employed by the
firms. It also outlines some of the real-world benefits and
challenges derived from the practices.

■ HONDA OF AMERICA: THE DEVELOPMENT OF A PRODUCT-ORIENTED NETWORK

How important is a lean supply system to the profitability of a company? Asking that question of any member of Honda's worldwide purchasing operation, one is likely to get an enthusiastic answer that sums up the corporate philosophy about the importance of suppliers in reducing manufacturing costs and improving product quality.

Honda's approach to supplier relations is rooted not only in the common Japanese practice of long-term supplier relationships, but also in its own history in the auto industry. Honda, like its Japanese counterparts, expects to maintain its relationship with suppliers for at least 25 to 50 years. However, unlike other Japanese auto makers, such as Toyota and Nissan, Honda's auto manufacturing tradition goes back only to the early 1960s.

When Honda, which had previously manufactured only motorcycles, entered the auto business, the company needed to develop its supply base from scratch, as MacDuffie and Helper explain.[2] It drew on three sources: suppliers of motorcycle parts, which were already familiar with Honda's business but had to learn to make automobile parts; other small suppliers in Japan, which needed to be persuaded to invest in new production capabilities for Honda; and larger companies supplying other Japanese auto companies.

Because the company's long-term corporate strategy requires making its products where they are sold and buying its parts where its products are made, Honda had to develop a base of American suppliers when it started operations in the United States. The motorcycle suppliers already in the Honda "family" were easiest to integrate into the new supply chain, as channels for coordination and technical assistance had already been established. Small local suppliers were eager to establish an affiliation with Honda but were technologically backward and unaccustomed to meeting the high quality and delivery standards required by an export-oriented automaker. These smaller suppliers needed considerable assistance in order to meet Honda's cost, quality, and service requirements.

The larger suppliers were primarily oriented toward their dominant customer, so Honda had to struggle to get them to be responsive. However, because they had more sophisticated technology and superior production expertise, Honda was forced to go to them for certain parts.

In setting up its North American supplier base, Honda first started with the small supplier companies located nearby its new manufacturing complex in Ohio. After the initial contacts with local suppliers were consolidated, Honda approached some of the larger auto suppliers whose primary customers were General Motors, Ford, and Chrysler. Although these larger suppliers had superior technological and human resources capabilities, they were not as responsive as Honda's smaller suppliers were. This made the development of these partnerships extremely difficult. From its experience in establishing its supplier relationships, Honda learned the importance of selecting suppliers that have adequate technological and personnel capabilities and that, above all, are willing to improve the auto maker's quality and lower the cost of products.[3]

Today, Honda of America Manufacturing buys almost 80 percent of the cost of every car from outside suppliers—amounting to $6 billion worth of goods from North American suppliers every year. From those purchased materials, Honda produces 620,000 vehicles and 900,000 engines. According to Dave Nelson, vice president of purchasing at Honda of America Manufacturing, "Since our 13,000 employees only make about 20 percent of the cost of the car, it is critical that we purchase well. We have about 800 people working with our 320 suppliers. About 300 of these people are in purchasing, about 200 are in quality, and about 300 are manufacturing and production engineers."[4]

To this end, Honda of America Manufacturing selects suppliers that are self-reliant, with a sufficiently diversified customer base that will allow them to continue to be in business if Honda of America Manufacturing's orders drop due to demand fluctuations. The importance of self-reliance was a lesson learned from painful experience during recessions in Japan, when Honda's commitment to its suppliers became a tremendous financial strain. Honda also selects suppliers that will be responsive to its manufacturing needs. Honda wants suppliers that are willing to take risks and invest in human resources and new technologies in advance of competitors.

In return, the selected suppliers establish a lifetime relationship with Honda of America Manufacturing, allowing them to forecast demands for their products more accurately. Thanks to Honda's sustained growth in the United States, Mexico, and Canada, Honda suppliers have experienced continuous growth in sales and product development.[5]

Because of its huge bottom-line impact, Honda of America Manufacturing's procurement group reports directly to the president of the company and occupies a strategic position at least equal to that of manufacturing. In addition, suppliers are regarded as an integral part of the company's strategic intent of manufacturing high-quality products at the lowest possible cost. According to Nelson, Honda of America Manufacturing works with suppliers in many different areas. Specifically, the Purchasing Division at Honda continually sets lower target costs for the most critical parts. In this way, if suppliers have problems reaching the cost targets, Honda helps them improve their productivity and reduce costs through value analysis and value engineering methods.[6]

Purchasing associates also aggressively attack quality problems, again helping suppliers as needed. Honda's goal is to achieve zero defects without having to inspect the suppliers' incoming parts. To this end, Honda has partnered with many suppliers in implementing quality circles. To establish a quality circle program at a supplier's plant, Honda associates meet with the supplier's top management members to explain the necessary training steps. Subsequently, the supplier takes the responsibility of the quality circle program by designating a quality leader within its organization. This strategy facilitates the implementation of a quality circle program best suited to the needs and cultures of diverse suppliers.[7]

In addition, Honda of America Manufacturing has developed a highly successful core-supplier development program called *BP*, which stands for Best Practice, Best Process, and Best Performance. Honda reported productivity increases averaging 50 percent at the 53 Honda suppliers participating in BP as of 1994. In essence, the BP program brings together people from Honda's multiple departments, for example, vehicle quality, process engineering, and the supplier's personnel, in order to solve routine problems related to manufacturing technology, work organization, second-tier suppliers, workforce training and compensation, and employment security.[8]

The BP program also focuses on long-term objectives. First, it encourages the supplier's fresh thoughts about Honda's production processes. Second, it allows Honda to gather data from external partners for more thorough and fact-based problem analysis. In addition, this data collection effort allows Honda to establish a more effective control of the suppliers' operations. Third, it generates commonsense, low-cost solutions by encouraging the elimination of root causes to problems in the suppliers' operations. Fourth, it fosters the development of Honda's knowledge of the suppliers' operations by arranging visits of Honda's BP representatives to the suppliers' manufacturing facilities. Finally, it strives to create a smooth flow of production upstream (at the suppliers' level) and downstream (within Honda) in the supply chain.[9]

Honda and its suppliers also partner in developing new car models. Purchasing actively interacts with suppliers in order to obtain feedback about its old models and improve its manufacturing performance for upcoming models. In addition, Honda promotes the suppliers' knowledge and technological capabilities by working closely with them to develop more efficient processes, find more efficient raw materials, and increase their order volumes. According to Takeshi Yamada, Honda of North America's president, "Our quality is the sum of the quality of our suppliers and the quality of our assembly." As Figure 3.1 shows, improvements in incoming parts have allowed Honda's operations in North America to reach quality levels far above the industry average. In 1995, Honda was recognized as the top-ranked auto manufacturer in the United States by the annual J. D. Power and Associates quality report. This quality study reported 70 problems per 100 Honda cars.[10] In addition,

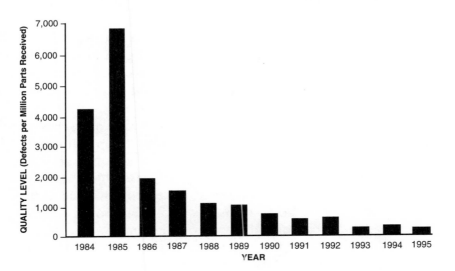

Figure 3.1 Continuous quality improvement.

Honda's Marysville, Ohio, manufacturing plant finished second in the plant category, with 62 problems per 100 cars, and the Honda Prelude (along with the Infinity J30) was rated the best model with only 48 problems per 100 cars.[11]

Honda's supply-chain management practices illustrate that partnering with suppliers to create lean supply systems requires an outstanding commitment. At the same time, it produces highly effective performance at both the supplier and customer level. Honda's experience also highlights important general lessons about supplier management.

First, firms must regard the acquisition of parts and raw materials as a process that covers both their purchasing and manufacturing activities. In addition, firms must regard the acquisition of parts and raw materials as an integral part of the firm's strategic intent. Second, customers must choose suppliers that not only have the technological and human resources necessary to meet the products' quality and cost specifications, but also are highly motivated partners. These partners must learn, make their operations totally accessible, take risks, and invest in technology and human resources to improve their productivity. Third, customers must manage the relationships with suppliers in a way that minimizes long-term dependence and speeds the transition to self-sufficiency. Customers must structure their suppliers' learning and productivity improvement process so that changes are easy to absorb. To this end, change process objectives must be concrete and easy to absorb. Furthermore, new approaches to productivity improvements must be highly reliable and must produce fast and visible improvements in suppliers' operations. Customers must transfer information and knowledge to the suppliers in a gradual fashion. The transfer should start in a single pilot area and diffuse to other areas of the organizations. Finally, customers must balance their need to monitor the suppliers' existing performance while encouraging them to learn new skills, which in the short term might disrupt that performance.

■ AMOCO CHEMICAL: TRANSFORMING DISTRIBUTION SYSTEMS TO INCREASE PERFORMANCE

The Amoco Corporation operates in more than 40 countries, in sectors ranging from petroleum and natural gas exploration, polymer, fabric and fiber manufacturing, and hazardous waste incineration, to medical diagnostic products and lasers.[12] Amoco Chemical (AC), one of Amoco's three industrial business areas, is in charge of the production of polymers, chemicals, fibers, and feedstock for worldwide export. Many of these products are bulk commodities whose prices fluctuate widely as a result of volatile demand and intense competition. These products also depend heavily on transportation and logistics operations, with transportation expenses comprising a large portion of their delivered cost.

The 1980s were years of important change in the oil industry. These changes were the result of the need to achieve greater efficiency and flexibility by eliminating imbalances between the upstream value chain (exploration and production) and the downstream value chain (refining, marketing, and chemicals). Amoco's major concern during the 1980s was to respond quickly to this ever-changing environment and to consolidate its position in the oil industry.

The importance of AC in the overall performance of the Amoco Corporation has increased over the last three decades. At the beginning of the 1970s, Amoco Corporation (then called Standard Indiana) began to emphasize the production of ingredients used in manufacturing processes and end-product manufacturing and distribution. By the end of the 1970s, the sales of chemical products accounted for about 7 percent of Amoco's earnings, and by the mid-eighties AC had also become a serious competitor in multiple fiber and fabric segments.

By 1991, however, Amoco's profitability began to trail other major competitors such as Exxon Chemical. The company realized it needed to act quickly to reverse this trend. It undertook a drastic reshaping of its marketing and logistics practices aimed at managing its worldwide network of assets more efficiently. Because this transformation was undertaken as part of a corporatewide restructuring, Amoco Chemical was able not only to streamline its processes, but also to align its objectives with those of other Amoco corporate business units.

As Figure 3.2 shows, Amoco Corporation currently is composed of 17 independent business groups that comprise three major sectors—Exploration and Production, Petroleum Products, and Chemicals. A major result of Amoco's transformation has been the realignment of quality control and the strengthening of its contact with customers. To this extent, three key goals have been accomplished:

1. The establishment of a customer-driven approach to quality.

2. The implementation of a method for measuring and managing customer satisfaction.

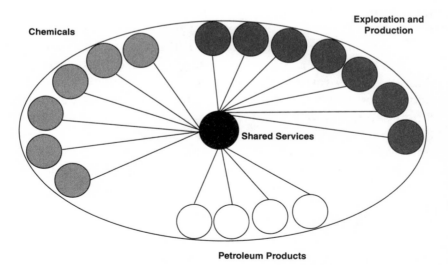

Figure 3.2 Amoco Corporation's organizational structure.

3. The recognition of the role that service plays in customer satisfaction and the competitive advantage derived from it.

Amoco also established a corporate strategic planning committee with each of the heads of the business groups as members. This committee serves as a forum to exchange ideas and concepts, and to assess new developments in Amoco's competitive environment. The result of this arrangement is an integrated strategic planning approach, fewer layers of management, quicker decision-making processes, and an integrated approach to quality throughout the corporation.[13]

Amoco Chemical's efforts paid off. The division now accounts for 15 percent of Amoco Corporation's sales and generates nearly 50 percent of its profits. In recent years, AC has focused its strategic objectives on broadening the chemical and polymer businesses, strengthening its operations, and further developing and globalizing its core businesses while diversifying its manufacturing operations into niche conversion and chemical businesses. To support its globalization initiative, AC has built a distribution network that is responsive to the customers' time, cost, and location utilities associated with AC's final products. AC is aiming to increase its current annual revenues to reach $10 billion per year by the year 2000. AC's infrastructure is made up of nine manufacturing facilities in the United States that move 115,000 shipments a year to 9,000 shipping locations. Of the 12 billion pounds moved on all modes each year, 40 percent (or 4.8 billion pounds) is classified as hazardous material.

According to Robert Theurer, AC's Director of Transportation and Marketing Services, the main element in the mission of AC's distribution unit is to "keep logistics in the line of sight and aligned with other strategic business unit objectives across AC and across the Amoco Corporation." To accomplish these goals AC organized its distribution organization into three nonoverlapping departments in charge of land transportation, marine transportation and export services, and transportation planning and support. These three divisions are all under the direction of a director of Transportation and Distribution (see Figure 3.3).

According to Theurer, AC designed its distribution system along four major principles:

1. *Optimize the physical planning and configuration of AC's logistics facilities.* To this end, AC assembled a global distribution network through joint venture agreements with companies abroad. This network arrangement has helped AC finance and revamp its distribution operations, while at the same time raised the firm's ability to optimize the use of its assets and effectively manage other logistics functions.

2. *Achieve an effective balance between centralization and decentralization* of distribution functions through a corporate office that provides a shared service to all AC strategic

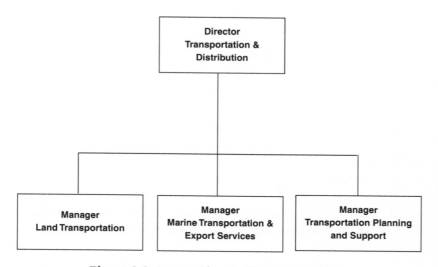

Figure 3.3 Amoco Chemical's transportation and distribution organization.

business units (SBUs). The SBUs are responsible for six independent product lines. However, they interact with the transportation and distribution unit through cross-functional teams of manufacturing and marketing specialists. According to Theurer, this arrangement is ideal because it integrates the firm's efforts and addresses cost-effectiveness factors across the firm's value chain. The SBUs are responsible for routine functions such as the reception and storage of finished products and raw materials. They are also responsible for market-specific functions such as the processing and fulfillment of customer orders and the forecasting of finished-product demand. In turn, the distribution department is organized along modal specialty lines, for example, land transportation (truck and rail) and marine transportation. These distribution units, along with the planning/support unit previously identified, are in charge of performing the necessary logistics training of the SBU personnel and interacting with the modal specialists on regulatory issues, rate negotiations, and carrier evaluations.

3. *Centralize transactional functions through a strategic information unit.* This unit is in charge of linking elements in the logistics system by centralizing and consolidating transactional functions that are essential to the movement of information throughout the firm's logistics infrastructure. Some of the transactional functions centralized include:

➤ Negotiation of all rates with rail, truck, and marine carriers.

➤ Tracking and payment of freight transportation by using automated systems that execute the bill of lading preparation and the order dispatching and accruals to payment. This system has a 100 percent coverage of all rail-related bills (which in turn account for 70 percent of *all* AC's shipments) and a 50 percent coverage of all truck-related bills.

➤ Developing leverage positions with carriers (e.g., asking customers to accept alternative modes so as to gain rate-negotiating leverage).

➤ Monitoring regulations and federal affairs.

4. *Acquiring major equipment and forecasting requirements for new equipment.* This capability has been central to the development of a flexible asset management system that allows AC to have equipment in place on extremely short lead times, and involves:

➤ Selecting and planning warehousing and terminal facilities.

➤ Auditing carrier safety, hazardous material terminal handing equipment and procedures.

AC realizes that long-term perspectives and continuous performance reviews are essential in maintaining a distribution system that effectively addresses the competitive needs of AC. To this end, AC started a long-term continuous improvement program to address customers' major complaints and needs.

AC also implemented an advanced supplier quality-qualifying program with 150 companies. As part of this program, AC consolidated its carrier base to 30 companies. Eight of those 30 carriers handle the lion's share of AC operations. The company also implemented a certification program in which carriers' quality and reliability are measured quarterly. This program has not only improved the performance of AC's carriers, but also has strengthened AC's relationship with its carriers by developing performance measures that have improved the way the carriers do business with other shippers. Finally, AC was able to implement a lump-sum freight payment program that has reduced costs by streamlining transportation payment processes. It also allows AC to take advantage of volume discounts and reduced rate variations.

◼ HARRIS CORPORATION: STREAMLINING LOGISTICS FOR COMPETITIVE ADVANTAGE

Founded in 1895, Harris Corporation has developed into a 27,000-employee worldwide company focused on four major businesses: electronic systems, semiconductors, communications, and office systems. Annual revenues in 1997 reached $3.6 billion. These revenues are derived from government (23%), industrial and consumer (77%) sales of major products in the areas of wireless and personal communications, digital television (DTV), healthcare records management, multimedia communications, automotive electronics, transportation communications, defense communications and information processing, and office document management. Furthermore, as explained by Philip Farmer, Harris's chairman of the board, president, and chief executive officer, in 1997,

> *Harris achieved record performance and posted its sixth year in a row of double-digit earnings growth. Orders, sales, net income, and earnings per share all reached record levels. Equally important, as its profitability has continued to increase, Harris has maintained an aggressive program of investing in the future. Expenditures for research and development and capital improvements have reached all-time highs and have been targeted to markets that offer Harris new opportunities for growth including digital television, wireless communications, and new applications for power-control semiconductors.*[14]

This impressive performance record did not come easy. A few years ago, Harris found itself in a very difficult financial condition. In 1991 Harris's four major businesses were under low-growth industry conditions and faced fierce competition from firms in the United States and abroad. Markets had fragmented and product lifecycles had shortened. In

1992, Harris's electronics systems and communications divisions barely managed to reach their targeted growth. Furthermore, the firm's office systems division reported substandard results for a third consecutive year. At that point Harris directors decided that major changes were needed.[15]

Harris's marketplace has changed to the point where dominating existing product segments was less important than being able to create new products and exploit them quickly. This more dynamic business environment required corporate strategy to become correspondingly more dynamic. Competition was now a "war of movement" in which success depended on anticipation of market trends and quick response to changing customer needs.

Harris realized that to be successful in such an environment, it needed to focus on hard-to-identify-and-develop products and services and hard-to-imitate organizational capabilities. To this end, Harris started by refocusing its competitive efforts. As Wesley Cantrell, president of the Office System Division, explained, "Our focus used to be `do what ever it takes to get the order.' Now our focus is `do whatever it takes to make the customer happy'"[16]. That change in focus allowed Harris to start emphasizing profits instead of sales volumes. The new perspective also underscored the need to earn customers' loyalty through rapid, reliable, and accurate product delivery. The customer focus ultimately generated a comprehensive reengineering process aimed at reducing operating costs by streamlining operations in all of Harris's divisions, from concept and design to delivery.

Logistics has played a crucial role in Harris's reengineering process. As Ray Jordon, transportation manager of Harris Corporation, explains, "The most important objective for Harris is to be a supplier easy to do business with. We are looking for quality above all. Our prime consideration is to deliver our products on time, with the requested specifications, and with no damages."

Accordingly, Harris consolidated transportation and materials-management functions into four Transportation

Management units (one for each of the four business units, e.g., Electronics, Communications, Semiconductor, and Office Systems). These management units are, in turn, part of a Traffic Council that aggregates corporatewide shipments, targets carriers and outlines strategies for rate negotiation. This logistics arrangement has eliminated the duplication that was rampant among Harris's shipping locations.

These improvements are reflected not only in $8 million in savings during the first eight years of operations, but also in a 99 percent on-time delivery rate of final products. Cycle time also improved dramatically. For example, the receiving process was shortened from eight days to 6.5 hours; the average time needed to distribute final products declined from three days to one day; and the time needed to review and inspect incoming parts fell from eight weeks to four days.

Each of the four transportation management units is in charge of controlling the use of carriers based on ongoing evaluations of quality performance. According to Jordon, the units emphasize not only monitoring and controlling transportation pricing, but also improving service levels, reducing cost, saving time, and increasing overall productivity. Harris representatives meet with carrier representatives every month to discuss ways in which both parties can improve the service provided to Harris's customers. According to Jordon, these sessions "routinely result in excellent solutions that are extremely valuable for both parties."

Harris's Transportation Management Units are also in charge of handling all shipment scheduling, routing, packaging, and documentation and tracking shipments through tie-ins to carrier real-time networks. Specifically, Harris has partnerships with Federal Express, United Parcel Service, and Airborne Express that provide direct access to the carriers' real-time tracking systems. These systems allow the company to monitor the delivery of up to 58 percent of its total annual shipments (equivalent to 200,000 shipments per year) that require overnight delivery.

In addition, Harris's Transportation Management Units monitor time-sensitive packages with a call-in system whereby carriers have to report in location every two hours and record their final arrival. They also control payments to carriers through electronic funds transfer and maintain EDI invoicing systems to bill government entities for contract work.

The evolution of Harris's logistics processes reflects the challenges that many engineering and technology-driven firms go through during the maturation of the competitive markets. The firm's experience illustrates the benefits of having a corporatewide understanding of the implications of managing supply-chain functions in an integrated manner. It also underscores the value of having an efficient integration of transportation and materials management responsibilities throughout different levels of the organization.

■ THE GAP: MANAGING PERISHABLE FASHIONS ON A GLOBAL SCALE

The Gap started in 1969, when Donald G. Fisher, its founder, came up with the idea of creating a clothing store that was the antithesis to the U.S. garment retailing industry at that time. The goal was to create a business that offered customers a wide variety of merchandise in an organized and easy-to-shop environment. The name "The Gap," the story goes, was an allusion to the generation gap prevalent in the 1960s.[17] After 29 years and as a result of cutting-edge supply-chain management practices, the name The Gap has become synonymous with exceptional performance in cycle-times, order-customer fulfillment, and logistics costs.

The Gap has become one of the world's most successful apparel manufacturing and retailing companies in the world. Indeed, 60,000 Gap employees have made possible an almost continuous increase in sales over the last ten years. In 1998, The Gap reported that its 2,237 retail stores worldwide sold $8.3 billion worth of clothing and accessories. This represents a 28 percent increase in annual sales with respect to 1997.[18]

Currently, The Gap has stores in the United States, Canada, the United Kingdom, France, Japan, and Germany. The Gap also has diversified its brand-name portfolio and now offers brands such as Gap Kids, Banana Republic, and Old Navy. Sales of these new product brands are conducted through 450 Gap Kids, 210 Banana Republic, and 140 Old Navy specialized stores in the United States. Operations in these stores are based on the same service quality underlying The Gap's operational founding principles.[19]

In 1996, Ro Leaphart, The Gap's senior director of logistics, made a presentation at the annual meeting of the Council of Logistics Management. In her presentation, on which the following description of the retailer's logistics operations is based, Leaphart defined The Gap as a "highly seasonal business." The Gap sells fashion, which by all accounts is a very perishable business in which products are simultaneously replaced and rotated eight times a year in stores around the globe. These products are transported over 7,500 trade lanes, 24 hours a day, seven days a week to the more than 2,000 Gap-owned stores worldwide.

Dealing with such a complex array of market, logistical, and even natural forces (a hurricane in Honduras once delayed T-shirt deliveries for an Old Navy promotional campaign) is a massively challenging undertaking. The Gap's secret, according to Leaphart, is to have a customer-driven, flexible inventory-management system in which the most pressing crises are solved on a daily basis and long-term strategies and policies are carefully planned and implemented with the collaboration of supply-chain partners.

The Gap's successful inventory-management efforts are supported by a small number of core realities:

1. *The Gap's supply-chain strategy is customer-driven.* The goal is to deliver what customers want, at the right place, and at the right time. To this end, The Gap has become a for-ward-integrated firm in which all 2,000-plus stores are exclu-sively owned by the firm. This forward integration has allowed the firm to manage its brand name effectively. In addition, it has played a central role in allowing headquar-ter's-based logistics specialists to source, plan, and schedule material movement from all corners of the planet. The Gap's logistics system has been configured to move materi-als in seasonal-flow patterns. An enterprise-resource-plan-ning system enables the retailer to pull finished products from the points of sale through its supply chain. This sys-tem allows the stores not only to receive products at the right time, but also to receive, according to Leaphart, "the yellow T-shirts with yellow socks, shorts, hat, and matching belt on exactly the same day, worldwide."

2. *The Gap's supply chain has an embedded operational flexibility that enables a cost-effective, time-driven, and accu-rate response to changes in customer demands.* Most of The Gap's product flows feature fashion items that may perish quickly, depending on fickle customer tastes. Compounding this challenge, stores can receive freight only during narrow windows of time, because they have very little stock space. Therefore, to make sure that carriers and the staff at the store coordinate deliveries in a cost-effective effective man-ner, The Gap has classified certain products into "basic mer-chandise" items, such as T-shirts, jeans, and crew-neck sweaters. These items are replenished on a regular basis and do not require special inventory management considera-tions. The retailer has classified other items, such as baby cribs, as "special merchandise." These items require cus-tomized logistics operations to reach final users.

3. *The company has configured a network of distribution centers that consolidate and distribute products in transit from the manufacturing centers to the stores.* In essence, these distri-bution centers receive and store products that are prepack-aged at the manufacturing centers. The distribution centers match these products against the orders from the stores, repack them, and ship them to "pullers" who distribute them to the stores or transship them to other distribution centers in a just-in-time (JIT) basis. Packaging and labeling the goods at the manufacturing-center level contributes to efficient organization of the supply-chain materials and finished products for final consumption at the stores. Packaging, labeling, and electronically recording the description of goods at the manufacturing-center level also allows inventory information to travel across the firm's supply chain.

This approach to managing information allows data to flow back and forth in an uninterrupted way from the points of origin (retailing centers) to the users (manufacturing centers). It results in a more accurate and efficient use of in-transit and demand-forecasting information, which is, ultimately, reflected in shorter cycle times and a synchronized use of human resources and capital assets.

4. *The Gap continuously works to keep its supply chain efficient and competitive.* The company uses performance metrics throughout its supply chain on a daily basis. This information monitoring allows The Gap to implement solutions quickly when problems arise, and develop ideas that will benefit its entire supply-chain system, not just an isolated area. For example, in managing inventories from its vendors around the world, the company constantly measures performance in delivery times, reliability, and costs throughout its supply chain. This allows The Gap to detect vendor inefficiencies and to correct them by solving the root causes or rotating vendors to improve overall performance.

Performance metrics are also critical in leveraging The Gap's transportation purchasing position around the world. In The Gap's view the company's logisticians are responsible for marginal costs in each of the firm's 7,500 trade lines. The goal is to monitor performance metrics to keep unit-costs down by reducing freight costs per unit. To fulfill this objective, The Gap gathers shipping data and leverages worldwide volumes to get better rates in small niche trade lanes where the rates to move only a few boxes can be astronomical. Such efforts are reflected in the products' profit margins. The Gap also reviews its main logistics processes every year. These annual reviews are possible because all processes are recorded in standard procedure manuals used by the entire organization. Third-party logistics providers also follow the standards and participate in creating the manuals and reviewing them annually. These reviews are feasible because the necessary information is collected in an accurate and timely way.

The company has developed core information systems that facilitate the frequent monitoring and control of logistics functions. These information systems enable information exchange between the logistics and other functional areas within the firm, such as finance and marketing.

5. *The Gap assembles crack logistics teams that create solutions and orchestrate practices.* These teams combine the complementary knowledge of people from diverse backgrounds. For example, when The Gap opened its stores in Japan, it assembled a group of specialists on real estate, outbound and inbound logistics, store operations, and marketing and finance. This group, according to Leaphart, was equipped to "address all the details involved in the developing of sound operational and strategic policies in a highly profitable, but highly unknown market, such as the Japanese."

Logistics teams are also assembled for longer-term purposes. For example, a group in information technology actively worked with The Gap retailing system and with The Gap's business partners to make sure that all parties had compatible and optimum EDI software and transmission capabilities. This activity has been crucial in the accurate use of transportation and inventory information.

6. *The Gap's international sourcing/distribution group is the centralized point of control for the movement of cargo* *worldwide*. This group expedites, to the extent possible, the customs clearance processes of goods originating at manufacturing plants overseas and of finished products entering markets abroad. In addition, the group negotiates freight rates for the entire organization. As Leaphart explained, this centralization allows The Gap to leverage its buying clout through volume purchases of finished goods from vendors, and through coordination of large volumes of cargo.

The Gap's logistics experience illustrates the extent to which customers influence the operations of supply chains. The way in which The Gap manages its inventory management infrastructure also demonstrates that firms can effectively combine their own and their supply-chain partners' resources to address both short-term and long-term challenges. The Gap's practices are also an interesting example of the way leading-edge logistics firms develop operational flexibility in their supply chains in order to use their logistics assets in a cost-effective way and accurately respond to customers in a timely fashion. In addition, The Gap's monitoring and controlling of its supply-chain's overall productivity is an illustration of the costs and benefits associated with an effective tracking of performance within all areas and across all members of the supply chain. Finally, it is also important to highlight The Gap's use of multifunctional teams to undertake both short- and long-term goals across its supply chain.

■ BECTON DICKINSON: MAKING THE TRANSFORMATION TO AN INTEGRATED STRATEGIC SUPPLY CHAIN

Becton Dickinson and Company (BDC) manufactures and sells medical supplies and devices and diagnostic systems for use by health care professionals, research institutions, and the general public. BDC is the leader in insulin injection systems, diabetes health care education, and disease management to improve treatment for people with diabetes. In addition, the company holds a strong market position in hypodermic needles and syringes and prefillable systems, and offers a wide array of safety products for medication delivery in many areas of the world. BDC is a world leader in the manufacture of evacuated blood collection systems. Furthermore, BDC is the leader in flow cytometry, an innovative technology that enables health care professionals to obtain new information on a wide range of immune system diseases, such as AIDS and Cancer. Finally, BDC manufactures products and instruments for infectious disease diagnosis.[20]

BDC's products, which must continually evolve to meet changing customer needs and market conditions, are manufactured at locations in the United States and abroad for sale worldwide. Non-U.S. operations represent nearly 50 percent of total company revenues. With annual revenues close to $3 billion, Becton Dickinson is focused on global businesses where it has demonstrated market leadership, positive contribution to patient care, potential for growth, and strong financial performance.[21]

BDC sees geographic expansion as a natural source of sales growth. Currently, BDC is strengthening its presence in two countries. The first country, China, has become one of the world's fastest-growing economies. It also has become a critical region for the manufacture and distribution of catheters and syringes for BDC. The second country, India, offers BDC the opportunity to participate in the improvement of the health-care practice of one of the world's largest middle-class sectors. BDC is currently close to opening a plant near New Delhi to manufacture several disposable products.[22]

➤ A Customer- and Supply-Chain-Centered Organization

Over the last 20 years, the health care environment has rapidly shifted as a result of changing demographics, increasing levels of international competition, the vertical integration of the health care industry and the rise of managed care as a common health care practice, and changing government regulations around the world. These market forces have caused BDC to commit itself to provide customers with technologically excellent products through coordinated, flexible, and fast processes. These pressures have also shown BDC the need to optimize the use of its resources by creating mutually beneficial partnerships with its customers—providing value that goes far beyond products and services.

To be able to establish such partnerships, BDC had to undertake a massive corporate reorganization that allowed it to improve its internal operational efficiency and its levels of customer satisfaction. In essence, BDC changed the way it did business. It realigned its organization and priorities to improve its ability to operate across divisions and functions—to reach its business partners and customers in a much more effective way. That effort resulted in the establishment of eight internal organizations. One of those eight organizations is Becton Dickinson's Supply Chain Services (BDSCS), a group charged with managing the fulfillment of the company's supply and service commitments to distributors in the medical device, laboratory, and pharmacy markets.[23]

In essence, BDSCS represents Becton Dickinson's commitment to streamline its internal processes and integrate its supply-chain activities in order to dispense logistics services to the other seven internal organizations. According to Nicholas J. LaHowchic, former president of BDSCS (LaHowchic left BDSCS to head supply-chain management for retailer The Limited), "BDC sees supply-chain management as an integrating process, used to create and sustain competitive advantage based on the delivery of basic and unexpected services." Alfred J. Battaglia, group president and chief information officer of BDC, emphasizes that "BDC is a product-oriented company in which logistics is the central axis of the corporate infrastructure. BDC is aware that making the best hypodermic syringe or blood collection tube is not enough.

In addition, it is important to create delivery systems that bring products to customers as swiftly as possible.[24]

Many logistics professionals are more likely to direct their work toward *facilitating* other organizational divisions' objectives. BDSCS, on the other hand, has gone a step further and focused on *integrating* the flow of materials and information throughout BDC's supply chain. The major mission of BDSCS is to be a leader in providing quality services and promoting supply-chain integration within BDC and between BDC and its distributors/channel partners and end-user customers.[25] The unit's specific goals are to provide one point of contact for each business partner, deliver products and information in an accurate and timely manner, efficiently manage inventories and logistics facilities, and establish more efficient procedures involving invoicing, credit collection, and contract administration. Using this approach, BDC has reduced operating costs by consolidating its administrative functions and integrating more effectively the use of its information technology capabilities. BDC's distributors/channel partners have also reduced their operating supply-chain costs by interacting with BDC through a single point of contact and by the use of complete EDI service coverage.

By fulfilling its organizational goals, BDSCS has also improved its asset utilization through considerable reductions in inventory levels and investments in fixed assets within BDC and across the supply-chain partners. BDSCS operations have increased corporate revenues by eliminating stockouts throughout the supply chain and facilitating BDC's expansion to new geographic and industrial markets.

➤ The Transformation Process

During an interview with Nicholas LaHowchic while he was still at BDSCS, he explained that implementing this type of supply-chain operation has meant addressing multiple internal factors. These factors include relocating people to new offices, implementing new information systems, creating new administrative policies, eliminating unneeded supply-chain facilities, and changing employee culture throughout the corporation. BDSCS took a comprehensive approach to creating this major logistics transformation as detailed below.

A Team Approach to Planning. The transformation process started in November 1994, when a cross-functional team of 21 BDC executives met to review what other companies had done in supply-chain improvements, and to decide what BDC should do. Several days later, the executive team, headed by LaHowchic, presented its findings to BDC's division presidents. At that time the team sought and got approval to create a new freestanding service company— BDSCS. "We believed the [new entity] should be a freestanding division, not a corporate support group. We wanted the division headed by a peer division president. The director should take over and manage the key supply-chain assets and expenses directly," LaHowchic explained.[26]

The new service division was designed to focus on distribution strategy and management, contract administration, rebate processing, customer service/order management, finished goods inventory management, accounts receivable/collections, and information technology. In January 1995, a core team was selected to oversee the restructuring of processes and practices throughout BDC. That team developed recommendations to undertake the transition process and established relationships from the current organizational structure to the new one. The team proposed an overall implementation strategy to ensure supply-chain integration.

Next, the change team reviewed all BDC's operations and developed an implementation plan and schedule. The team identified projects that needed to be done, and charted the projects on a quarter-by-quarter basis over two years. In each area being redesigned, the team first looked at what leading companies in logistics were doing. For example, when addressing customer support, they studied L.L. Bean and the GE Customer Support Center. The team also created new practices or policies for the BDC companies being supported (e.g., new conditions of offering, new terms of sale, etc.). In addition, they developed new returns management processes and redesigned contract pricing and collection procedures.

Maintaining Customer Service During the Change Process. An important issue in the change process was to ensure that change could be made without destabilizing processes that affected customers. To this end, LaHowchic's group moved the traditional customer service activities into BDSCS before they were reengineered. "This enabled us to stabilize the function within our organization first to make sure there was no negative impact on the customer," said LaHowchic.

Integrating Information Systems. Subsequently, BDSCS integrated BDC's flows of information. To this end, LaHowchic and his team converted the old customer service processes into a new call center concept that allowed a single point of contact for all customer questions, orders, technical/sales support, billing, records management, returns authorization, and so on. BDC also updated its information systems in order to support BDSCS. At the start of this effort, none of BDC's divisions used the same technology platforms. "We needed to upgrade to a newer platform and get all the divisions electronically integrated where they were not before," LaHowchic remembered. "We had to make a significant investment in hardware and software, and move hundreds of people into a single new space dedicated to information systems."

In October 1995, BDSCS started this systems upgrade. By January 1996, just 90 days later, the company had relocated about 230 people to the new workspace. They were up and running on a new systems platform that integrated each division's existing system into a larger umbrella system. This umbrella system makes information in the individual division system universally available. "This is like the cockpit for the whole organization," LaHowchic explains.[27]

Keeping the Organization's Eyes on the Prize. Once the preliminary stage of establishing the framework for the transformation of BDC's supply chain was over, the remainder of the process came through relatively quickly. By mid-1997, forecasting, inventory management, contract administration, and order processing and fulfillment activities had all been transferred under the BDSCS umbrella. Some of these changes entailed substantial planning and coordination efforts. This is why, according to LaHowchic, it was critical to "get the entire organization to focus on the work and the processes relentlessly, without worrying about past organization structures and processes. If you are not careful, you will end up with people defending what they have done in the past. That is not the point. We have to consider what is important for the customer, effective productivity and leveraging utility and resources."[28]

Continuing to Envision the Future. While the changes at BDC were not completed at the time of the author's interview, the company had high hopes for its new supply-chain approach. BDSCS's goal, says LaHowchic, is to become an enterprise that:

➤ Provides high levels of service quality in supply-chain activities with distribution/channel partners and product divisions.

➤ Leverages administrative transaction activities for distributors/channel partners and product divisions.

➤ Provides cost-effective physical infrastructure for product divisions.

➤ Develops and implements service products for distributors/channel partners and international divisions.

➤ Is acknowledged by distributors/channel partners as a supplier of choice for having created value through its service offerings.

These goals are simple to define but hard to execute. In order to accomplish them, BDSCS is evolving to become a functional division that fully integrates BDC's organizational capabilities.[29]

■ JOHNSON & JOHNSON: LOGISTICS PERFORMANCE BENCHMARKING

Johnson & Johnson (J&J) has more experience with global supply-chain management than many other firms. That experience allows it to take a longer-term view and evaluate more carefully the benefits associated with the reorganization of its supply-chain infrastructure. A critical element in J&J's supply-chain management practices is centralization. As its business has become more global, J&J has centralized the management of its distribution of raw materials and finished products. In the past, J&J's subsidiary companies used to handle their own distribution. The company changed this practice about 15 years ago, after customers complained of difficulty in controlling shipments from J&J plants. "It was advantageous to have all the orders come to one place so we could consolidate them into one shipment for the customer. By combining volumes, we generated substantial savings in freight rates," Axel O. Velden, director of J&J's Export Division, commented.[30]

Another interesting element in J&J's logistics operation is the establishment of Johnson & Johnson Health Care Systems (J&JHCS), a strategic logistics unit dedicated to continually improving the firm's logistics efficiency, achieving high profit margins, and consolidating J&J's market share position in the industries in which it competes. J&JHCS's current organization dates back to 1982 when John Buck, Jr. and Richard Velten, two veterans of J&J's logistics operations, created a headquarters-based core group of nine people. Today, this group makes commercial decisions and manages shipments for 35 J&J strategic business units. It handles products ranging from disposable contact lenses to sterilization equipment.[31]

J&JHCS was initially established under the name of Johnson & Johnson's Hospital Services in order to help J&J's Professional Companies respond to the demands and needs of the health care industry, particularly hospitals and distributors. At that time, according to John Buck, J&JHCS's manager of Transportation Provider Relations, "we were a very difficult company to do business with because there was no centralization. J&J's customers had to deal with at least a couple dozen J&J business groups. So, in order to make it easier for the customer to do business with J&J, we created a `single-stop-shopping' entity to provide customers with one point of contact for all the array of products and offerings J&J had. At the same time," Buck recalls, "we were trying to maximize our ability to consolidate the use of our human, physical, and financial resources."

Over the course of 13 years, Hospital Services has implemented a customer-driven process-improvement effort designed to contain costs, improve productivity, and increase efficiency. Hospital Services has bundled a wide array of logistics services including distribution, order handling, billing, shipping, and collecting—all provided through a network of five regional distribution centers across the United States. As of 1994, this service unit processed an estimated

650,000 shipments per year to 12,000 customer destinations across the United States.

In 1995, Hospital Services developed into Health Care Systems. Hospital Services served as an internally oriented entity that facilitated efficient operations. The evolution to Health Care Systems reflected a need for this group to become a corporate integrator of supply-chain activities across multiple J&J functions, as well as across suppliers and customers. Today, Health Care Systems is a Johnson & Johnson strategic business unit, oriented primarily toward adding value to the service provided to J&J's customers. It accomplishes this by streamlining and managing the flow of goods and information across the supply chains of 35 J&J Business Groups.

According to Buck, in the next five years "J&JHCS aims to become a best-in-class supplier of products and services to J&J's customers. In addition, J&JHCS wants to become the primary logistics contractor for all J&J companies. We will do this by differentiating ourselves from outside third-party logistics providers through the offering of customized consulting and services to J&J's business groups." Buck is also quick to point out that this evolution will not be a smooth ride. "There is constant change in our products' marketplaces." He explains:

> We anticipate major changes in our customers' requirements as a result of significant consolidations of our customer base. The whole health care industry, in general, is also changing as more firms shift to managed care. And we're seeing more consolidation among the various major hospital buying groups. These users are positioning themselves into groups with extremely large buying power. Our ability to respond to them in a proactive way while still making money will be critical to our future success.

Indeed, Buck explains that, like many other supply-chain and logistics professionals, he must be able to achieve returns on investment that meet shareholders' expectations. He does this by constantly generating new sales dollars and reducing costs through effective allocation of J&JHCS's resources across J&J's supply chain. To this end, J&JHCS employs a continuous benchmarking process to build its supply-chain infrastructure and capabilities. This, according to Buck, is a customer-oriented process that involves core supply-chain competencies in the areas of transportation, inventory management, materials management, and customer service.

Each month, Buck's group benchmarks the performance and processes in core activities in these supply-chain areas. This effort involves all J&JHCS departments and J&J's corporate directors. "The process," he explains, "starts by developing a baseline that will allow the firm to position itself with respect to other stakeholders in its industry." In other words, the firm will be able to establish its position with respect to the rest of the playing field (e.g., its competition, and how its performance compares against its customer expectations).

A well-conducted benchmarking process is also an ideal way to identify the firm's strengths and weaknesses. Finally, a well-conducted benchmarking process allows the firm to direct its improvement efforts, and decide whether to adopt a continuous-improvement process approach or make radical business changes in order to close performance gaps or jump ahead of the initially established benchmarks.

To baseline its operations, J&JHCS starts by measuring performance levels in supply-chain areas such as transportation operations, inventory management, materials management, and customer service. Subsequently, J&JHCS compares its performance against historical performance data, the performance of other J&J Business Groups, the performance of third-party logistics providers, and the performance expected by J&J's end customers. "In outbound transportation," says Buck, "the customer is actually the best source to evaluate performance measures. To this end, we ask our distributors to measure in a number of areas how we perform against their other suppliers. Specifically, we evaluate our shipping accuracy in order to set parameters for distribution center efficiency and invoicing accuracy. For internal transportation, we have about 18 different measurements. We consider key areas such as order fill rate and percentage of orders not complete."

With respect to inventory management, J&JHCS' distribution center (DC) and inventory groups measure cycle counting and inventory turns at the DC level. In addition, these groups measure inventory weeks on hand, and measure inbound lead-time replenishment times. With respect to materials management, J&JHCS maintains standards for handling incoming and outgoing product cases for all J&J's product groups. "We know the costs for major operations," Buck notes. "All these costs result from activity-based costing methodologies that allow us to baseline DC operations. We have identified all the costs associated with every individual process or function."

On the external front, Buck reports that the company measures customer service order accuracy (percent of orders delivered with errors), as well as carrier delivery accuracy. J&JHCS also measures its total order cycle time against previously agreed-upon commitments to customers. "Where there are exceptions," he notes, "we measure our claims processing against standards for response time—both internally and for customer problem resolution."

Overall, Health Care Systems measures virtually everything it does against predetermined performance standards. In addition, the business unit constantly updates its improvement goals to keep them current with changing conditions.

The baselining information is critical to identifying gaps with respect to J&JHCS's performance standards, and with respect to the performance of competing firms. J&JHCS accomplishes this comparison by separating supply-chain processes within its core groups (internal processes), and supply-chain processes that cut across sup-pliers and customers (external processes). The identification of performance gaps of internal processes relies on previously set period goals. For external processes, J&JHCS compares its performance to that of third-party logistics firms. "Relying on third-party logistics providers to identify performance gaps is part of a corporate initiative to contin-uously challenge the position of J&JHCS within J&J," explains Buck. "What happens typically is that J&J's senior management asks `Why do we or don't we use third-party logistics companies?' We are always looking at how we com-pare against them on costs, opportunity, and service perfor-mance. We also have to keep differentiating ourselves on an operating basis. J&JHCS is a `third-party logistics provider' for the J&J Company. If we do not provide a better and a more customized noncore service to J&J, we will not be needed. That is why this continuous `insourcing/outsourc-ing challenge' is useful. It allows us to determine, on a process-basis, if a third-party provider would add value above and beyond what we can."

The final step of the process involves planning how to close the performance gaps. To this end, J&JHCS prioritizes which deficiencies to address by analyzing their impact on J&J's bottom-line numbers (i.e., profit margins, market share, and revenue growth). For example, J&JHCS routinely tracks the impact of many transportation performance indices on operating costs. In addition, order cycle times are constantly correlated to inventory levels.

Conversely, J&JHCS does not monitor the impact of more subjective performance components—such as order fill rates—on bottom-line performance because the effects that such measurements have on J&JHS revenues depend mainly on customer needs. This does not mean that J&JHCS does not monitor its order fill rate performance at all. As Buck points out, "Having a perfect order fill rate does not mean that we will make more money or get more business. But not measur-ing order fill rate could result in having no sales."

J&JHCS is positioning itself to be the leader of the pack in logistics services, rather than a follower. Consequently when the company benchmarks its performance against other firms, it not only measures current performance, but also measures predicted performance. "This practice gives us a point of reference," notes Buck. "It allows us to know where we have gone historically and where we have to go."

Overall, benchmarking is a vital tool and source of information for J&JHCS. "We are constantly trying to understand how our customers evaluate performance and perceive our service," he concludes. "This gives us a clear picture of our opportunities for improvement. It also helps us avoid over-servicing or overperforming, or, by the same token, under-performing in cases where higher levels of service are expected."

Chapter 4

The Outsourcing Megatrend

Earlier chapters have defined the extended enterprise and discussed its origin as a response to the global economy that has emerged during the 1980s and 1990s. This highly competitive environment dictates that companies place a premium on speed to market and quick, flexible customer response. Indeed, "with delivery speed, not price, often winning the sale, many companies are focusing attention on logistics as the next management frontier," according to Noel Greis and John Kasarda, writing in a recent article published in the *California Management Review.*

As a result, logistics systems have become an integral part of the new competitive model. Products must be delivered to markets not only in a timely way but with "personalized features, point-of-delivery customization, and value-added services."[1] Furthermore, the production processes to support this delivery system require just-in-time receipt of components with minimum inventories. This approach maximizes a company's ability to assemble parts precisely when they are needed to satisfy specific customer requirements.

Highly responsive logistics systems place a premium on speed, flexibility, accuracy, and precision. They require sophisticated management information systems capable of sharing data in real time among suppliers, manufacturers, warehouses, carriers, and customers. Important features of the new logistics system include linked databases, paperless transactions, analytic modeling systems, and real-time tracking and tracing systems.

Increasingly, however, firms are realizing that the requirements of today's effective logistics systems exceed both the capabilities of their current logistics staff and the resources now allocated to the function. Furthermore, the current pace of technology makes it difficult for many firms to keep up with the latest developments. As a result, outsourcing—contracting with outside firms to provide needed functions and services—has emerged as a viable option for operating logistics systems.

This chapter initially explores logistics outsourcing as part of the overall management trend toward outsourcing. It then presents 10 prominent reasons firms decide to outsource logistics functions and offers case studies to illustrate the approaches they have taken—from incremental, function-by-function outsourcing to a total outsourcing of all logistics functions. Next, the chapter evaluates what in-house logistics capabilities a firm needs to manage and monitor outsourcing partners. The focus then turns to another critical part of the equation: the third-party logistics provider network and how it is evolving and changing in response to the needs of the marketplace. Experiences with this network show that not all results have been positive; in fact, some have been quite disappointing. The chapter concludes by summarizing the overall trends in logistics outsourcing to date.

■ THE RATIONALE FOR OUTSOURCING

The traditional view of an "organization" is rooted in the post–industrial revolution model, defined by giants such as

General Motors and DuPont in the 1920s and 1930s. In this model, an organization is assumed to own and manage directly most, if not all, of its required resources, and business success is synonymous with acquiring the factors of production.

Over the years, however, as organizations have become more complex, their resources likewise have become further specialized and directed toward various elements of their operations—product design, engineering, manufacturing, human resources, information technology, logistics, and sales, just to name a few. This specialization opened the door to outsourcing non-core activities, challenging executives to reevaluate the desirability of traditional vertical integration and meeting all needs with in-house support.

The potential advantages of a much more flexible organization based on core competencies and mutually beneficial, longer-term outside relationships soon became clear. In the global economy of the twenty-first century, almost any organization can gain access to resources. What differentiates companies now is their intellectual capital, knowledge, and expertise, not the size and scope of the resources they own and manage. As a result, firms across the corporate spectrum are choosing to outsource a variety of functions, both to allow them to focus on core competencies and to take advantage of the skills and leverage of outsourcing partners in noncore areas. No firm is too large or too small to consider outsourcing.

In addition, current competitive conditions are forcing many firms to revise their priorities and focus resources on a few key activities. Products or services that provide unique marketplace differentiation and represent the basis of competitive advantage continue to be owned by the firm. Rightly so: These are critical to success or failure. However, by subcontracting non-core items or functions to external suppliers, management can leverage its resources, spread its risk, and concentrate on issues critical to survival and potential growth. Non-core functions frequently outsourced include, among many others, information technology, human resources, training, market research, and logistics.

The impetus for subcontracting logistics is multifaceted. First, the reengineering and rightsizing of American business during the mid-to-late 1980s thinned both the number and the skill level of corporate operations groups. At the same time, some forward-thinking retailers and manufacturers began to change business practices on the supply side of the supply chain, introducing progressive, time-based competitive strategies such as just-in-time (JIT) and Efficient Consumer Response. These initiatives increased the complexity of supplier networks from procurement through the movement of raw materials and raised the level of customers' quality and service expectations.

Fundamental changes also occurred during this time in the technology used by logistics system providers—for example, computers, satellite communications for real-time information to track freight and vehicles, new information systems, analytic computer models, and real-time data/information sharing. Finally, following deregulation, the transportation provider network began to provide an increasingly more sophisticated, dependable, and cost-efficient set of services.

Perhaps the most important and least recognized reason for the increase in popularity and perceived value of third-party logistics services is the awareness that outsourcing can help a company gain market advantage by better managing its external environment. Interactions with third-party partners are a valuable source of information and data about their markets. With this data, they can perform thorough competitive assessments and establish valid industry benchmarks. Exchanging information with supply-chain partners can also expand a firm's knowledge of local and regional markets and give them expertise in new processes, ideas, and technologies.

■ TEN PROMINENT REASONS FOR OUTSOURCING

Through a series of studies conducted since 1991 (including surveys of over 1,200 companies), ongoing work with its members, and ongoing reviews of other major studies, the Outsourcing Institute has developed a clear understanding of the reasons companies outsource various activities and the potential benefits to be gained.[2] These potential benefits include the following:

1. Improve company focus

2. Gain access to world-class capabilities

3. Accelerate reengineering benefits

4. Share risks

5. Free resources for other purposes

6. Make capital funds available

7. Create a cash infusion

8. Reduce and control operating costs

9. Gain access to resources not available internally

10. Deal effectively with a function that is difficult to manage or out of control

While these are reasons for outsourcing any function, they also apply to logistics. The following discussion addresses the logistics implications of these 10 reasons in reverse order to emphasize another important Institute finding: Outsourcing is a long-term strategic-management tool. When the strategic reasons for outsourcing are overshadowed by short-term business concerns, companies are often disappointed with the results. Looking at the 10 reasons, then, we can label items 6 through 10 as tactical—meaning they affect the day-to-day operation of the business. Items 1 through 5 are more long range and strategic. They drive where the company is headed and how it will get there. Outsourcing, studies show, works best when firms adopt a long-range, strategic approach.

➤ Reason 10: Deal Effectively With a Function that Is Difficult to Manage or Out of Control

One reason for outsourcing is to bring better operating controls to a function that currently is difficult to manage or is "out of control." Indeed, managers may perceive their logistics systems to be difficult to manage if they are consistently failing to meet customer delivery expectations or their just-in-time shipments are consistently late, forcing closure of many production facilities due to lack of materials.

Nevertheless, outsourcing may not be a viable solution even in such cases, if the organization does not initially examine the underlying causes of the logistics failure. If the organization does not understand the requirements, expectations, or needed resources for logistics systems, then its ability to communicate problems to an outside provider will be severely limited. Furthermore, without a clearly defined set of expectations, the outsourcing partner will find it difficult to solve problems and, as a result, will be unsuccessful.

In short, the first step in using outsourcing to gain control of the logistics process is to determine how the system has failed and to create a general approach for solving the problem. Managers will be disappointed if they simply throw up their hands and turn the logistics systems over to an outsourcing partner.

➤ Reason 9: Gain Access to Resources Not Available Internally

Companies may outsource their logistics systems because they do not have access to the required resources within the company. For example, to minimize logistics costs best practices logistics systems use sophisticated analytic models for production and warehouse location as well as shipment size, mode, and carrier selection. Many companies do not have the expertise to implement such models without turning to outsourcing partners. Furthermore, best practices logistics systems require sophisticated information systems to enhance real-time communication among customers, suppliers, manufacturers, and carriers. Through outsourcing, companies can quickly and perhaps less expensively implement logistics information systems they would otherwise have to build from scratch.

➤ Reason 8: Reduce and Control Operating Costs

The single most important tactical reason for outsourcing any activity is to reduce and control operating costs. The cost advantage comes from access to the outside provider's lower cost structure, which may be the result of economies of scale or some other advantage based on specialization. Similarly, several studies indicate that cost reduction and service improvement are the primary reasons that firms outsource logistics functions.[3-6] In addition, companies that try to update their logistics systems to best-in-class on their own may incur higher research, development, marketing, and deployment expenses than they would if they outsourced the job. These costs would need to be passed on to the customer.

➤ Reason 7: Create a Cash Infusion

Outsourcing often involves the transfer of assets from a company to its new logistics provider. Equipment, facilities, vehicles, and licenses used in current operations all have a value and can, in fact, be sold to the outsourcing partner. In operating its own logistics system, for example, the company may have acquired a sophisticated electronic data interchange system, a fleet of vehicles for private carriage, or a set of warehouses, all of which can be sold to the outsourcing partner—often for a substantial amount of cash. The outsourcing partner can then use these assets to provide logistics services to the client partner and, frequently, to other clients as well.

➤ Reason 6: Make Capital Funds Available

Outsourcing is a way to reduce the need to invest capital funds in non-core business functions. Instead of acquiring resources through capital expenditures, a company can contract for them on an "as used," operational expense basis. As a result, capital funds are more available for core areas. Outsourcing can also improve certain financial measurements of a firm by eliminating the need to show return on equity from capital investments in non-core areas. In most organizations, competition for capital funds is tremendous, and deciding where to invest them is one of the most important senior management tasks. However, when a firm contracts out for its fleet vehicles, buildings, or computers, these areas no longer compete for the company's capital. Often, these types of investments have been difficult to justify anyway, when compared to areas more directly related to creating products or serving the customer.

When assessing the capital investments needed to reach best-in-class logistics systems, a significant investment is often needed in areas such as computer systems, software packages, communications systems, and information systems. However, these expensive assets may have a very short shelf life, since new technological developments can quickly make them obsolete.

➤ Reason 5: Free Resources for Other Purposes

Every organization has limits on the resources available to it. The constant challenge is to ensure that limited resources are expended in the most valuable areas. Outsourcing permits an organization to redirect its resources from non-core activities toward activities that have a greater return in serving the customer. Most often, the resources redirected through outsourcing are employees. By outsourcing non-core functions, the organization can redirect these people, or at least the staff slots they represent, into greater value-adding activities. People whose energies are currently focused internally can now be focused externally—on the customer.

Indeed, many of the firms who have outsourced their logistics systems have reduced their logistics personnel requirements as well. The outsourcing partner either hires some or all of the company's logistics staff or finds alternative personnel with updated skill sets.

➤ Reason 4: Share Risks

All of the investments an organization makes carry risks. When companies outsource they become more flexible, more dynamic, and better able to change themselves to meet changing opportunities. Markets, competition, government regulations, financial conditions, and technologies all change extremely quickly. Keeping up with these changes, especially when each one requires a significant investment of resources and dollars, is very difficult, and "bet your company" types of investments are all too common. Outsourcing is a vehicle for sharing these risks across many companies. Outsourcing providers make investments not on behalf of just one firm, but on behalf of their many clients. By sharing these investments, the risks borne by any single company are significantly reduced.

Developing state-of-the-art logistics systems requires significant investments and entails great risk. It now appears, for example, that many of the sophisticated electronic data interchange (EDI) systems that have been developed for communication and data exchange systems between shippers and carriers will become obsolete and replaced by Internet-based communications and data-exchange programs. Furthermore, the current generation of software to design a firm's supply chain will likely be replaced within the next five years. Instead, a completely different system that is real-time and Internet-based will link suppliers, manufacturers, carriers, distributors, and customers in a real-time, shared-data system for data interchange, transactions, and communications. Individual firms attempting to develop and manage systems by themselves will encounter significant risk and a high probability of failure. The outsourcing alternative, with shared risk, seems a much more viable option.

➤ Reason 3: Accelerate Reengineering Benefits

Outsourcing is often a byproduct of another powerful management tool: *business process reengineering.* Reengineering is the fundamental rethinking of business processes, with the aim of dramatic improvements in critical measures of performance such as cost, quality, service, and speed. Taking an internal function to world-class standards can require a lot of executive time. More and more companies are deciding to outsource the functions that can immediately guarantee the improvements offered by reengineering but without the risks. Outsourcing becomes a way to realize the benefits of reengineering today instead of tomorrow by having an outside organization—one that is already reengineered to world-class standards—take over the process.

Reengineering has also taken place in corporate logistics systems. It encompasses a shift to the use of analytic models for sourcing of raw materials, location of manufacturing plants and distribution centers, and selection of shipment sizes, modes, and individual carriers. As noted above, it also involves installing elaborate information systems linking suppliers, manufacturers, distribution centers, carriers, and customers in real time. These shared databases allow for transfers of information for billing, payments, ordering, and acknowledgment of shipment receipts. The reengineered systems require new hardware, software, and retraining of key personnel. The selection of a world-class outsourcing partner facilitates the entire process.

➤ Reason 2: Access to World-Class Capabilities

By the very nature of their specialization, outsourcing providers can bring extensive worldwide, world-class capabilities to meet the needs of their customers. Just as their clients are outsourcing to improve their focus, these vendors have honed their skills for providing specialized services. Often, vendor capabilities are the result of extensive and long-term investments in technology, methodologies, and people. In many cases, the vendor's capabilities include specialized industry expertise gained through working with many clients facing similar challenges. This expertise may be translated into skills, processes, or technologies.

The providers of logistics outsourcing services have aggressively advanced their services around the world by developing strategic alliances with local firms. In addition, they have assembled highly effective distribution technology and information systems to improve the cost efficiency of logistics systems, harnessing the tremendous advances in both the hardware and software available to manage logistics systems. Furthermore, world-class outsourcing firms have been improving information systems, which now allow real-time shared information among suppliers, manufacturers, carriers, distributors, and customers. As a result, firms that outsource logistics can have the latest and most advanced systems without having to make the initial investment in these systems on their own.

➤ Reason 1: Improve Company Focus

Outsourcing allows firms to focus on broader business issues while having operational details assumed by an outside expert. For many companies, this is the single most compelling reason for choosing this option. As operational issues take increasing amounts of management's time and attention or become stuck in middle management "decision gridlock," resulting financial and opportunity costs can negatively affect the organization's future. By outsourcing non-core functions, the organization can focus on core processes that lead to competitive advantage, accelerating growth and success.

Similarly, for firms in which logistics systems have not been identified as a core competency, outsourcing can lead to strategic advantage. The overall logistics costs of the firm can be lowered, while customer service is enhanced. The outsourcing solution gives the firm access to new technology and new approaches, proven to improve service and lower costs in a wide variety of situations and applications.

■ COMPARING IN-HOUSE CAPABILITIES WITH OUTSOURCING ALTERNATIVES

Deciding whether to outsource initially or to continue out-sourcing is a complex make-or-buy decision. Before even considering the option, experts recommend that companies conduct a thorough objective audit or appraisal of existing logistics operations, including a realistic assessment of current capabilities/limitations and future logistics needs. Outsourcing may be viewed as a very effective approach when compared to an inefficient in-house logistics operation. However, it may not be as attractive compared to a restructured, efficient, internal logistics operation.

Once the audit is complete, a company can establish a set of objectives against which various outsourcing alternatives can be compared and measured. Outsourcing should always be evaluated as an alternative to an in-house solution. A 1996 report by consulting firm A. T. Kearney, entitled *A Shipper's Approach to Contract Logistics,*[7] suggests that buyers ask themselves the following questions when considering whether to outsource:

➤ How is the "industry standard" performance changing in terms of cycle times and service levels?

➤ How should I improve my logistics operation in terms of speed, cost, or customer service?

➤ Are my competitors outsourcing? What approaches have they taken?

➤ Do I have the capability to make radical changes to my logistics operations?

➤ Do I have the volume to develop new capabilities cost effectively?

➤ Are there secondary benefits to developing an in-house capability? Are the skills transferable to my core business?

On the basis of the answers to these questions, firms may elect to manage logistics *activities in-house* and not pursue the outsourcing alternative. However, if a firm selects the outsourcing alternative, various approaches are possible. One is to outsource a limited number of specific logistical functions/activities. Candidate functions/activities include logistics information systems, carrier selection/rate negotiation, shipment planning, fleet management, warehousing/operations, freight payments/auditing, inventory management, packaging, order processing, and product returns. The firm may decide to outsource one or more of these initially and contract out for others after becoming more familiar with the process. This *incremental approach* to logistics outsourcing allows firms to gain some experience prior to a full commitment to logistics outsourcing. It contrasts with an alternative approach of *outsourcing the entire logistics system at one time.*

The following section presents examples of firms fitting into each of the three categories.

➤ Keeping Logistics Services In-House

As indicated in Chapter 3, Johnson & Johnson, which manufactures a broad array of medical and personal care products, has resisted the current rage to outsource logistics services to third-party providers. While Johnson & Johnson continuously updates its supply-chain management, the company's logisticians believe some traditional processes are not worth changing for the trend of the moment. J&J's executives feel that they can handle many logistics functions better than a third party.[8]

As its business has become more global, Johnson & Johnson has moved to centralized management of its distribution of raw materials and finished products. Its subsidiary companies used to handle their own distribution. This practice changed about 15 years ago, after customers complained of difficulty controlling shipments from multiple Johnson & Johnson plants. Johnson & Johnson found it advantageous to have all the orders come to one place so it could consolidate them into one shipment for the customer. By combining volumes, the firm generated substantial savings in freight rates.

Johnson & Johnson's export division has a logistics staff of 46, which manages international customer service and transportation as well as accounting and information systems. The export division supplies overseas plants and distributors with finished goods, work-in-progress for local packaging, raw materials, and machinery. It also arranges special packaging for different regions of the world.

As a longtime leader in the global field of health care products, Johnson & Johnson has accumulated an extensive logistics asset base that allows it to effectively manage its supply chain worldwide—with no need for outsourcing at this time.[5]

Like Johnson & Johnson, Ericsson Network Systems, a Stockholm-based telecommunications equipment manufacturer, still keeps firm control over its supply-chain management. Executives believe that when a company has full control of the logistics process, it has a better chance to avoid bottlenecks in the supply chain.

Ericsson manages its U.S. logistics, including imports and exports, with a 14-person group based in Richardson, Texas. The company decided to handle all distribution from Texas and expects growth to increase the logistics staff to 25. By improving its internal processes, Ericsson reduced handling costs for cellular phones by more than half and customs clearance for some cargo into Texas from five days to three hours.

➤ The Incremental Approach to Logistics Outsourcing

The North American Logistics Services (NALS) unit of candy manufacturer Mars, Inc. provides advanced logistics services and information for Mars, with the goals of improved customer satisfaction and supply-chain integration that create a competitive advantage. An alliance with Cass Information Systems allows NALS to deliver timely and accurate logistics cost information. To create this information, the alliance links transportation and warehousing payment data with customer and supplier databases and order entry systems to give NALS a view across its supply chain. This enables NALS to create a logistics cost database that supports financial reporting, tactical decision making, and even some strategic initiatives such as network modeling.[9]

The alliance between NALS and Cass also incorporates the function of freight payment and auditing. NALS purchases more than $1 million in logistics services each day. Cass audits, processes, and pays over half a million individual transactions a year. In effect, Cass is an extension of NALS's accounting, finance, management information systems, and logistics departments. Since the Mars/Cass alliance was first formed, Cass has processed 3.2 million freight bills for $1.4 billion, and has given Mars the information it needs for logistics management, planning, and strategy.[10]

Between April 1990 and October 1993, PPG Industries, Inc. of Pittsburgh gradually converted its private fleet to a dedicated contract carriage operation, hiring Schneider National to take over the operation. One of the primary reasons that PPG turned to outsourcing was concern over liability issues. PPG's fleet carried large quantities of hazardous materials. In view of the many large awards to plaintiffs involved in accidents, PPG was no longer comfortable shouldering the risk exposure. Today, the outsourcing alliance between PPG and Schneider National saves PPG $500,000 a year, and Schneider handles about 30 percent of PPG's truckload business.[11]

In 1995, Dole Foods restructured its warehousing network and outsourced its last two internal warehouses to third-party logistics providers. Dole measures the performance of each of its warehousing providers with a report card using an extensive set of performance measures. The third-party logistics providers supply Dole with a 30-day "Board of Directors" report that details statistical data by employee, function, and building.[12]

➤ The Total Approach to Logistics Outsourcing

Poor logistics is one of the major reasons that Laura Ashley, Inc. recorded a dismal business performance from the late 1980s to the early 1990s. The company's decision to outsource its entire global logistics operation to Business Logistics Services (BLS), a division of Federal Express, enabled a gain of over $1 million in total profits in 1992.

Under the 10-year contract, BLS manages all aspects of the flow of goods and information within the retailer's supply chain, from routing and transport to global inventory management and global consignment tracking. In the short term, implementation of the new logistics system helped reduce Laura Ashley's stock levels by allowing just-in-time shipments. Other important benefits include improved customer service and improved reliability, speed, and frequency of deliveries. Senior management at Laura Ashley believes that the agreement gives the company access to management systems and logistics capacity that it could never develop itself.

■ THE THIRD-PARTY PROVIDER SECTOR AT A GLANCE

The growth of outsourcing has created significant opportunities for firms that specialize in providing logistics services, known as third-party providers. A third-party logistics firm is an external supplier that performs all or part of an organization's logistics functions. The total volume of logistics business handled by third-party providers has grown appreciably over the past several years. For example, the total volume of contract logistics activity grew from an estimated $10 billion in 1992 to $25 billion in 1996. Today, 20 percent annual growth rates are the norm for third-party logistics providers.

In 1992, an estimated 374 firms provided contract logistics services, with business volume capturing 2.7 percent of the available logistics activity. By 1996, the number of providers had increased to 421 and the penetration rate to 6 percent of the available business. By 2000, the number of providers is expected to increase to 474 and the volume of business is predicted to increase to $50 billion, achieving a 10 percent share of the total logistics business, according to Robert V. Delaney, senior vice president with Cass Information Systems. Delaney monitors ongoing logistics trends and developments, and reports on them each year in a press conference presentation given in Washington, D.C.

The level of business interest in contract logistics is also clear from corporate logistics managers' responses to a recent international survey conducted by educators Robert C. Lieb, Robert A. Millen, and Luk N. Van Wassenhove concerning the use of these services. In an article published in the *International Journal of Physical Distribution and Logistics Management*[13], the authors noted that about 46 percent of U.S. managers and 78 percent of Western European managers reported an extensive or moderate commitment to the use of third-party logistics services.

While many third-party providers are small niche players, the industry has a number of large firms as well. Examples of the latter include FedEx Business Logistics Services, UPS Worldwide Logistics, Exel Logistics, Caliber Logistics, Menlo Logistics, Schneider Logistics, Emery Worldwide Global Logistics, Ryder Integrated Logistics, GATX Logistics, and Caterpillar Logistics Services.

The relatively young third-party provider market is continuing to evolve and mature. Initially, most third-party logistics services providers came from the for-hire transportation sector. Building on their existing partnerships with shippers, these carriers (predominantly motor) expanded into a wider spectrum of logistics support activities. More recently, technology-driven (rather than asset-driven) third-party logistics providers have emerged. These companies act as total supply-chain systems integrators, and apply their systems expertise, decision-support models, and supply-chain optimization software to manage the supply chain across their clients' global operations.

Today, contract logistics providers are attempting to offer customized services driven by customer needs and based on value. For example, since Caliber Logistics began in 1989, the firm has won contracts for a broad range of services such as inventory management, warehousing, cross-docking, product assembly and logistics information systems. Another third-party firm, Menlo Logistics, recently announced agreements on six major projects expected to generate more than $1.15 billion in revenue over the next five years. Menlo's new partnerships, which encompass international operations and integration of logistics functions across the entire supply chain, are with Intel Corporation, IBM Corporation, Haworth Inc., H.B. Fuller Company, and Ingersoll-Rand Company. "These partnerships are significant for the contract logistics industry because they prove that manufacturers from a cross-section of industries worldwide have discovered how logistics expertise can improve their profits," commented John Williford, president and CEO of Menlo Logistics.

In addition, the number of specialized industry-specific third-party logistics providers is growing. Examples include Chemical Lehman Logistics servicing the chemical industry; Johnson & Johnson Logistics Services handling the health care industry; IBM Logistics Services for the computer parts business; Caliber Logistics for the high-tech, industrial, retail/consumer, health care, and automotive industries; and Mellon Logistics Services, a Gillette spin-off, for the consumer products industry. These providers gear their capabilities to meet the specific requirements of their client industry.

All these developments ensure that the third-party logistics market will continue to experience rapid changes and shakeouts. This instability has important implications for companies using third party services. Indeed, while the third-party providers are increasingly offering more sophisticated products and services, there is greater variance in the quality of their services and in the stability of their operations. The next section discusses some ramifications of the unsettled status of the third-party provider market.

■ EXPERIENCES WITH THIRD-PARTY PROVIDERS: POSITIVE AND NEGATIVE

Overall, the evidence regarding the impact of logistics outsourcing has been incomplete and anecdotal and has not been systematically quantified. A few studies suggest some important benefits. For example, Lieb, Millen, and Van Wassenhove reported survey results from 131 large U.S. manufacturers and 73 large Western European manufacturers. The logistics outsourcing benefit most noted by U.S. managers was cost reduction. In contrast, the European managers most frequently cited flexibility as a benefit, with cost reduction and better cost control as the second-most-often mentioned. Some Western European managers noted cost reductions of from 30 to 40 percent as a result of their logistics outsourcing activities. In a recent study by Lieb and Randall of the 500 largest American manufacturing firms, 92 responded. Of that total, 38 percent reported that lower cost was a benefit of using third-party providers of logistics services.[11] Perhaps the observed growth in third-party logistics outsourcing is the best evidence of its advantages.[14]

In the absence of more data—and a careful assessment of in-house versus outsourcing options for logistics—firms cannot assume that outsourcing will automatically yield benefits. The recent very messy divorce between Ryder Integrated Logistics and Office Max illustrates some of the pitfalls of outsourcing. Office Max sued Ryder for failing to meet expectations. Ryder responded with a countersuit, charging that Office Max misinterpreted the contract and was wrong in its accusations. Clearly, both parties had different expectations about the results of the outsourcing arrangement.

Other users of third-party logistics provider services report being disappointed with the long-term outcomes of their relationships. Initially, these companies experienced a significant boost (in the double digits) in productivity or performance—during the first months of a contract. After that, the gains tapered off, and the third party was hard pressed to replicate the initial boost.

Here again, a lack of understanding appears to be at the root of the disappointment. Regardless of the situation, it is imperative that contract logistics providers and their customers work together to write a clearly worded contract that fully spells out contractor duties as well as client expectations, and also details how performance will be measured during the relationship.

■ ADOPTING A SYSTEMATIC APPROACH

While this chapter has documented the basic rationale behind the increasing use of logistics outsourcing by firms, it is clear that a number of unanswered questions remain. To ensure a positive experience, each firm that considers outsourcing logistics must systematically gather data to assess the options, develop an outsourcing strategy, and identify and select an appropriate outsourcing partner. The firm also needs to be precise about contractual expectations with its outsourcing partner and to monitor performance regularly. Finally, companies should specifically, and, where possible, quantitatively, document the impacts of the logistics outsourcing partnership—what benefits or inadequacies occur.

To help fill the gaps in information about the third-party logistics phenomenon, the authors have conducted the largest, most comprehensive systematic assessment of the logistics outsourcing experience to date. Chapter 5 provides a detailed report of the results of that effort, which both support and add to the discussion in this chapter. Chapter 5 also presents a list of outsourcing best practices drawn from survey respondents' experiences.

Chapter

5

Outsourcing Best Practices

Although a company that outsources logistics functions no longer has to perform them, it still must manage the process and the partnership effectively to achieve desired benefits. As Chapter 6 pointed out, the success of outsourcing agreements depends heavily on the management skills of the firms engaging the services of third-party providers. Because outsourcing has become a more widely used management option, logistics managers have gained more experience and learned what management practices are most successful. Results of our recent survey, featuring the responses of 500 corporate logistics managers experienced in outsourcing (including 114 Fortune 500 companies), capture that experience and offer important insights into real-world management issues and strategies.[1] Based on these results, this chapter provides an overview of corporate wisdom and experience regarding:

➤ Making the decision to outsource

➤ Developing strategies and approaches to logistics outsourcing

➤ Selecting logistics providers

➤ Structuring a contract with the chosen firm(s)

➤ Assigning responsibility for managing third-party providers

➤ Monitoring and measuring performance

➤ Sustaining a productive relationship

➤ Evaluating business gains from logistics outsourcing, including competitive advantage, customer service levels, and overall logistics costs

In addition, this chapter discusses the benefits that companies in the survey experienced from logistics outsourcing and offers a summary list of logistics outsourcing best practices.

■ THE RESEARCH METHODOLOGY

Researchers from the University of Maryland Supply Chain Management Center sent a survey instrument to 11,571 logistics managers across the United States identified as having outsourced one or more logistics functions. In addition, the team conducted 17 in-depth interviews with managers from companies identified in the literature or by major third-party logistics providers as having engaged in logistics outsourcing. The main objective of the interview process was to validate findings from the survey analysis. The survey instrument included four sections with questions on the following topics:

➤ Section 1: The extent of outsourcing and the patterns of logistics activities outsourced.

➤ Section 2: The decision to outsource, including the best ways to identify and select an outsourcing firm.

➤ Section 3: The best practices in managing and monitoring a third-party relationship, including the identification of necessary contract provisions.

➤ Section 4: The service, cost, and competitive gains from third-party contracting.

All questions in the survey (except for those requesting descriptive information) used a five-point scale for responses. For example, respondents were provided with a list of potential benefits from outsourcing and were asked to rate each of these benefits on a five-point scale from very effective (rating of one) to very ineffective (rating of five).

The survey was sent to all names on *Transportation and Distribution* magazine's "outsourcing" list and a follow-up notice was sent one week after the initial mailing.[2] The research team received usable surveys from 463 respondents.[3] The response rate (4.32 percent) is in line with expectations from mass mailings but is lower than the rate obtained by most academic studies. The low rate may have been due to the very detailed nature of the survey. Despite the low response rate, the total number of surveys returned represents, to the best of our knowledge, the largest database of respondents to an outsourcing survey.[4] The number was more than sufficient to support a variety of statistical tests. Among the survey respondents were logistics managers from 21 of the top Fortune 50 and from 35 of the Fortune 100 companies.

To test for potential nonresponse bias (i.e., the respondent group not resembling the nonrespondents on the mailing list), researchers compared characteristics of the firms employing survey respondents to those in the population of firms represented by the *Transportation and Distribution* list. This comparison showed that a higher percentage of the survey respondents represented large firms (as measured by the number of employees) as compared to the population of firms.[5] As a caution, therefore, results are more likely applicable to larger firms than smaller firms.

Survey respondents also provided information on their company's SIC codes (i.e., Standard Industrial Classification). Approximately 70 percent represented companies in the manufacturing segment, with an additional 10 percent in the wholesale trade group and 7 percent in the retail trade group. The sample distribution closely resembled the population of 11,571 managers. Figure 5.1 provides a list of survey respondents by industry.

The 17 in-depth interviews focused on particularly important issues with logistics outsourcing, including the insourcing versus outsourcing decision process. A discussion of interview results is integrated into the presentation of the survey results.

■ MAKING THE DECISION TO OUTSOURCE

Logistics managers overwhelmingly believe that they need their own people to evaluate in-house costs and processes in order to assess the potential advantages of outsourcing (Figure 5.2). For example, survey respondents said that use of in-house personnel was five times more effective than the use of consultants or third parties to make comparisons between third-party providers and company processes and costs. As a vice president for Corporate Services of a major manufacturer of semiconductors explained in an interview, "The start of the outsourcing process is a clear understanding of a company's processes and costs. A firm does not have to know how to fix the problems in its supply chain, but it has to understand the problems." However, consultants and third parties may be "somewhat effective" in mapping processes and identifying/benchmarking costs or activities, according to mail survey respondents. Figure 5.2 compares the effectiveness of different approaches to assessing the potential benefits of third-party logistics providers.

Industry Segment	Number of Respondents
Mining	3
Construction	1
Manufacturing of food and kindred products	41
Manufacturing of tobacco products	1
Manufacturing of textile mill products	5
Manufacturing of apparel products	9
Manufacturing of lumber and wood products	4
Manufacturing of furniture and fixtures	13
Manufacturing of paper and allied products	16
Printing and publishing	13
Manufacturing of chemical products	31
Petroleum refining	1
Manufacturing of rubber and plastic products	13
Manufacturing of leather products	4
Manufacturing of stone, clay, glass, and concrete products	5
Manufacturing of primary metal products	17
Manufacturing of fabricated metal products	21
Manufacturing of industrial, commercial, and computer equipment	36
Manufacturing of electronic and electrical components	41
Manufacturing of transportation equipment	18
Manufacturing of measuring, analyzing, and controlling instruments	17
Manufacturing of miscellaneous products	10
Transport, communications, electric, gas, and sanitary services	13
Wholesale trade	40
Retail trade	27
Service industries	7
Public Administration	3
Number of respondents not reporting their SIC codes	53
Total	463

Figure 5.1 Breakdown of survey respondents by industry.

Rating by various parties: How effective are they at comparing company costs with outsourcing charges?

	Very Effective	Somewhat Effective	Neither Effective nor Ineffective	Somewhat Ineffective	Very Ineffective
			% of Respondents		
Company personnel	54.4	36.1	6.4	2.4	0.7
Outside consultants	11.3	50.8	27.3	6.5	4.1
Third-party providers	10.6	39.6	26.1	16.9	6.8

Rating by various parties: How effective are they at comparing company processes with outsourcing processes?

	Very Effective	Somewhat Effective	Neither Effective nor Ineffective	Somewhat Ineffective	Very Ineffective
			% of Respondents		
Company personnel	48.9	35.9	10.7	3.8	0.7
Outside consultants	13.5	50.5	26.8	5.5	3.7
Third-party providers	13.2	42.9	26.0	13.2	4.6

Figure 5.2 Effectiveness of various parties in comparing company and third party costs and processes. (*Source:* University of Maryland Supply Chain Management Center, *Logistics Outsourcing Survey, 1997.*)

What are the reasons companies decide to outsource some or all logistics functions? Survey results reinforced the findings reported in Chapter 4: For most companies the desire for cost savings dominates and is the leading driver of outsourcing efforts. Indeed, 41 percent of respondents said the best explanation for their company's decision to outsource was the high cost savings or revenue-enhancing potential of outsourcing. In addition, 26.5 percent of respondents claimed that they had opted to outsource logistics functions primarily because these functions were not part of the firm's core capabilities. Clearly, respondents are aware that focusing on core business processes and outsourcing non-core activities can be a more efficient use of internal resources. Other reasons given for logistics outsourcing include its being an element of a strategic redesign of the entire supply chain and its identification as a major problem area for the company.

■ DEVELOPING STRATEGIES AND APPROACHES TO LOGISTICS OUTSOURCING

The survey questioned logistics managers about the number of individual logistics functions outsourced and the average length of time each function has been outsourced. Based on a list of functions provided, respondents indicated whether each function was currently outsourced, previously (but not currently) outsourced, or likely to be outsourced in the future (Figure 5.3).

Responses on this topic show four major patterns of outsourcing employed by the respondent firms:

1. Not currently outsourcing any logistics functions (19% of respondents).

2. Outsourcing incrementally—one function at a time (23.5% outsourced one logistics function, while an additional 19.9% outsourced two functions at the time they filled out the survey). This incremental approach to outsourcing focuses attention on specific deficiencies and the need to fix those problems.

3. Outsourcing two or three functions and then leaping to total supply-chain management outsourcing to try to get system-gains.

Function	Currently Outsourcing		Not Currently Outsourced But Expect to Outsource in the Future		Previously, But No Longer Outsource	
	Number of Respondents	% of Total Respondents	Number of Respondents	% of Total Respondents	Number of Respondents	% of Total Respondents
Freight payments and auditing	264	57.0	42	9.1	18	3.9
Warehousing and operations	134	28.9	53	11.4	5	1.1
Carrier selection and rate negotiation	110	23.8	54	11.7	27	5.8
Information systems	91	19.7	62	13.4	8	1.7
Shipment planning	81	17.5	50	10.8	7	1.5
Fleet management	78	16.8	31	6.7	12	2.6
Packaging	71	15.3	35	7.6	4	0.9
Product returns	70	15.1	47	10.2	4	0.9
Order processing and fulfillment	48	10.4	27	5.8	4	0.9
All supply chain functions	46	9.9	43	9.3	6	1.3
Inventory management	37	8.0	42	9.1	4	0.9

Figure 5.3 Past, current, and future trends in the outsourcing of logistics services. (*Source:* University of Maryland Supply Chain Management Center, *Logistics Outsourcing Survey,* 1997.)

4. Starting with total supply-chain outsourcing, based on an assessment that the sum of savings and advantages from total outsourcing is greater than that of its parts (9.9% of respondents).

Firms taking approach 4 have likely made a corporate decision not to include logistics among their core competencies. As a result, they evaluate the outsourcing decision from a comprehensive systems viewpoint.

Study results show that firms appear to have the longest average outsourcing experience with more routinized logistics functions, including warehousing operations (8.6 years), packaging (7.8 years), order processing/fulfillment (7 years), and freight payments/auditing (6.6 years). More recently outsourced functions/systems include those that are more planning intensive and require more dynamic modeling. These include inventory management (5.4 years), logistics information systems (4.4 years), and carrier selection/rate negotiation (4.4 years).

A surprisingly large percentage of firms are outsourcing these more planning-intensive functions. In fact, 19.4 percent of respondents outsource logistics information systems, and 23.5 percent outsource carrier selection/rate negotiations (Figure 5.3).

Why are firms outsourcing these planning intensive functions? The relatively high levels of outsourcing suggest that more and more shippers are becoming aware of opportunities inherent in the effective use of information in supply chains. Indeed, among survey respondents, over 13.4 percent indicated a future possibility to outsource the logistics information systems function, 11.7 percent the carrier selection and rate negotiation function, and 10.8 percent the shipment planning function. Another probable reason for the popularity of carrier selection/rate negotiation outsourcing is increasing competition in the transportation provider network. An explosion of new services and rate complexities has created new, more complex choices for shippers; outsourcing can help reduce the decision-making burden while improving the selection and negotiation processes.

Continuing high levels of outsourcing for warehousing operations reflect the increasing sophistication of warehousing procedures and automation systems. Warehousing may not be a core capability in many firms, and outsourcing can help rationalize assets and achieve necessary economies of scale while avoiding sunk costs during periods of extreme demand volatility.

Clearly, then, outsourcing logistics functions is widespread among the respondents and will continue to grow according to respondents' indications of future intentions. In addition to the respondents that currently outsource all of their supply-chain functions, 9.3 percent of our sample firms note that they may outsource all functions in the future.

It is important to note, however, that 12.5 percent of respondents had to make critical changes and take previously outsourced functions back in-house. Although this percentage is significant, only 4.1 percent of total respondents have stopped outsourcing completely and are no longer using any services of third-party logistics providers. In some functions, such as carrier selection and rate negotiation, a relatively high proportion of respondents (5.83 percent) have opted to take outsourced logistics functions back in-house. One of the likely reasons for this decision is the increasing availability of moderately priced logistics information technology, which can provide capabilities in-house that may have previously been available only through an outside firm. In addition, firms may outsource a particular function in order to learn from the outsourcing firm. Once they have absorbed the third-party knowledge, they may choose to bring the activities back in house.

■ SELECTING LOGISTICS PROVIDERS

As indicated in Figure 5.4, in-house research appears to be the most effective information source for identifying potential third-party logistics providers. (Figure 5.4 illustrates what means survey respondents used to identify candidate third-party logistics service providers.) In-house logistics capability, including practical skills and computer tools, is

Source	Very Effective	Somewhat Effective	Neither Effective nor Ineffective	Somewhat Ineffective	Very Ineffective	Rank 1	Rank 2	Rank 3
			(Percentage of Respondents)					
In-house research	43.5	42.6	9.0	4.2	0.6	49.4	18.3	9.4
Trade associations	10.2	52.6	28.5	7.1	1.6	5.2	13.0	20.3
Consulting firms	9.9	46.8	28.6	10.6	4.1	6.5	15.3	16.5
Professional networks	37.6	44.1	14.9	2.7	0.7	27.3	28.3	17.0
Trade journal articles	8.6	45.0	34.8	8.9	2.7	2.7	9.3	10.4
Vendor advertising	5.8	25.6	44.4	18.4	5.8	1.5	3.3	8.1
Conferences	14.0	43.3	31.2	8.8	2.7	4.0	10.3	17.0

Figure 5.4 Effectiveness of sources for identifying third-party providers. (*Source:* University of Maryland Supply Chain Management Center, *Logistics Outsourcing Survey, 1997.*)

critical in evaluating and selecting third-party logistics providers. Professional networks (i.e., word of mouth) are another important way to identify outside logistics firms. However, respondents rated third-party logistics advertising as the least effective source of information.

The bottom line is this: Companies rely more on sources of information that are close to their immediate business activity circles and that have no vested interests or biases in providing the information. In general, when making the outsourcing decision and selecting partners, firms tend to have more confidence in internal assessment staff than in external suppliers of information and imported techniques.

Another selection parameter has to do with the characteristics of the third-party logistics provider itself. Figure 5.5 lists what users of third-party logistics services perceive as the most important attributes. As Figure 5.5 illustrates, financial stability is a critical attribute for third-party logistics providers. In fact, it was rated a very important selection factor by a higher percentage of the respondents than any other characteristic. An overwhelming majority of respondents also perceived customer service capability and price of services to be very important. On the other hand, respondents rated the third-party logistics provider's human resources policies and a company's prior relationship with the outsourcing firm as significantly less important than any other attributes.

Several inferences emerge from these results and the findings from our interviews. First, firms appreciate attributes that reduce risks and contribute more significantly and quickly to bottom-line goals. For example, financial stability, customer service capabilities, and price of services are more important than attributes offering longer-term benefits that are harder to measure and improve (e.g., general reputation, problem-solving creativity, compatibility with company culture and philosophy, information systems and technology capabilities, and reputation for continuous improvement). Second, attributes associated with the scope of the third-

Attributes	Very Important	Somewhat Important	Neither Important nor Unimportant	Somewhat Unimportant	Very Unimportant	Rank 1	Rank 2	Rank 3
			(Percentage of Respondents)					
Owns assets	22.0	42.8	25.5	5.5	4.2	2.7	4.0	3.5
Price of services	66.1	31.7	2.0	0.0	0.2	31.3	17.7	15.0
Size	10.7	55.7	27.1	6.1	0.4	1.0	1.2	2.7
Human resources policy	10.4	35.8	41.1	9.5	3.3	1.0	1.2	1.2
General reputation	48.6	43.4	7.2	0.9	0.0	8.2	7.5	10.0
Financial stability	72.8	24.6	2.4	0.2	0.0	12.4	17.2	19.0
International scope	17.7	37.6	29.7	9.6	5.5	1.7	1.5	2.8
Problem-solving creativity	59.2	34.5	5.2	1.1	0.0	9.0	11.0	11.0
Compatibility with company culture and philosophy	44.8	38.4	14.0	2.6	0.2	9.2	9.5	7.2
Prior relationship with company	12.9	37.5	37.7	8.3	3.7	0.5	1.2	0.5
Information systems and technology capabilities	54.2	37.7	6.1	1.8	0.2	6.0	12.2	12.0
Customer service capability	72.5	22.7	3.9	0.7	0.2	14.7	12.5	11.0
Reputation for continuous improvement	47.1	43.4	8.5	1.1	0.0	1.2	2.7	5.5

Figure 5.5 Perceived importance of third-party logistics providers' attributes. (*Source:* University of Maryland Supply Chain Management Center, *Logistics Outsourcing Survey,* 1997.)

party logistics provider (e.g., size, asset ownership, and international coverage) are significantly less important than all the other attributes, with the exception of human resources policies and prior relationship with the outsourcing company. Companies pay less attention to the provider's human resources policies than to any other attribute, although, as some of the executives interviewed explained, it is important to include all critical stakeholders in the client company and the provider firm in the selection process.

■ STRUCTURING A CONTRACT

Results in Figure 5.6 highlight the importance of various provisions to be included in a contract with a third party provider.

"Cost of services" is perceived as the most necessary provision in a contract. Fully 78.6 percent of respondents stated that a cost of services provision was very necessary to include in a contract with a third party provider. Other provisions that were considered to be among the most necessary to include in a contract were "performance metrics," "delineation of duties," "termination clause," and "insurance allocation of liabilities."

Companies appeared to see provisions related to the management of human resources as significantly less necessary than any other. In our detailed interviews, however, executives were divided on this question. Some of the executives recommended including joint contract stipulations that allow for the transferring, relocation, and retraining of internal logistics personnel. Others indicated that the third-party logistics provider itself should take sole responsibility for providing the necessary personnel to run the outsourced operations.

Survey respondents also perceived that sharing financial gains was significantly less necessary than most other provi-

Provision	Very Necessary	Somewhat Necessary	Neither Necessary nor Unnecessary	Somewhat Unnecessary	Very Unnecessary	Rank 1	Rank 2	Rank 3
			(Percentage of Respondents)					
Length of contract	45.1	37.9	12.5	3.7	0.9	6.1	8.4	10.4
Payment method	43.8	38.5	15.6	1.3	0.7	3.4	7.4	6.0
Gainsharing	20.7	40.7	30.9	4.7	3.1	4.2	5.9	4.7
Delineation of duties	54.1	32.4	11.8	0.9	0.9	23.1	13.8	8.4
Cost of services	78.6	20.5	0.9	0.0	0.0	37.1	25.4	13.6
Dispute mechanisms	35.3	51.3	10.7	1.8	0.9	0.7	4.2	7.7
Noncompliance penalties	33.9	46.8	15.5	3.1	0.7	2.2	3.7	6.0
Human resources	13.2	32.0	41.5	9.9	3.3	0.7	1.0	3.0
Technology/intellectual property	29.3	44.3	19.8	4.8	1.8	2.2	4.4	7.7
Insurance/allocation of liabilities	51.8	30.8	15.4	1.8	0.2	3.4	7.4	8.6
Termination clause	52.5	35.2	11.2	0.9	0.2	0.7	2.0	11.2
Performance metrics	56.3	34.3	8.6	0.7	0.2	16.0	16.0	12.7

Figure 5.6 Perceived necessity of various contract provisions. (*Source:* University of Maryland Supply Chain Management Center, *Logistics Outsourcing Survey, 1997.*)

sions. This result may reflect respondents' belief that strong control over the relationship with a third-party logistics provider is significantly more critical to achieving joint benefits.

■ WHO MANAGES THE THIRD PARTY?

Once a contract between a company and a third-party logistics provider is in place, another important management task arises: establishing within the company a managerial person/group to take charge of the relationship on an ongoing basis. Figure 5.7 presents survey results regarding the most effective corporate approach to managing the relationship. The favored option: entrusting contract management to a chief logistics officer (CLO), who has a specialized skill and authority and can be very effective in building and maintaining strategic focus and oversight. The other management options proposed (a non-CLO senior executive; a cross-functional headquarters (HQ) team; a cross-functional strategic business unit (SBU) team; a HQ/SBU team; and outside consultants) had far fewer proponents.

From these results, it would appear that firms perceive that assigning centralized oversight by a single logistics expert is the most effective way to manage the relationship with a third-party provider. The chosen manager must have a clear understanding of the companywide logistics system and decision-making power at the executive level of the organization. Figure 5.7 outlines how survey participants responded to the question of what works best in terms of who manages the third-party logistics provider.

Furthermore, an important part of the CLO's function in managing the third-party relationship is the need to compare and evaluate the benefits of outsourcing versus insourcing on a continuous basis. For example, one interviewee from a chemical company initially determined that logis-

Alternatives for Provider Oversight	Very Effective	Somewhat Effective	Neither Effective nor Ineffective	Somewhat Ineffective	Very Ineffective	Rank 1	Rank 2	Rank 3
			(Percentage of Respondents)					
Chief logistics officer (CLO)	52.8	26.0	14.7	3.3	3.3	51.5	9.1	9.3
Senior executive (non-CLO)	15.2	36.3	30.7	11.5	6.2	7.6	24.8	12.1
Cross-functional headquarters (HQ) team	20.6	41.7	26.6	6.9	4.1	11.9	19.7	27.0
Cross-functional strategic business unit (SBU) level team	22.2	38.1	28.7	7.7	3.3	10.6	24.8	19.4
Cross-functional HQ/SBU team	21.7	37.9	29.2	8.2	3.0	12.1	16.8	22.5
Outside consultant	2.4	16.2	40.7	24.5	16.2	1.0	2.1	8.7

Figure 5.7 Who is best-equipped to manage the third-party provider? (*Source:* University of Maryland Supply Chain Management Center, *Logistics Outsourcing Survey*, 1997.)

tics activities at one of its distribution centers should be outsourced to a third-party provider. However, based on the ongoing analysis of the results from outsourcing as well as ongoing evaluation of the company's internal capabilities, he subsequently decided to take back control of this distribution center. This change led to the following improvements regarding outsourcing performance:

➤ Storage space utilization was improved 20.3 percent

➤ Inbound receiving costs improved 22.6 percent

➤ On-time delivery of customer orders' shipping timeliness improved 73.9 percent

➤ Productivity (cartons/hour) improved 16.3 percent

➤ Cost per carton handled improved 9.2 percent

➤ Freight costs as a percentage of sales improved 7.7 percent

■ MONITORING AND MEASURING PERFORMANCE

Having assigned management responsibilities for a company's relationship with a third-party provider, it is critical to develop methods to monitor that relationship. Extensive use of metrics is the most favored approach (see Figure 5.8). Over 65 percent of respondents rated "performance metrics" as very effective in monitoring the performance of third parties. The next most effective method was "joint review meetings." These were rated very effective by almost 60 percent of respondents. Only 10.8 percent of respondents believed that audits by outside consultants were very effective in monitoring third-party logistics providers' performance—the lowest rating of all the monitoring methods.

Monitoring Methods	Very Effective	Somewhat Effective	Neither Effective nor Ineffective	Somewhat Ineffective	Very Ineffective	Rank 1	Rank 2	Rank 3
			(Percentage of Respondents)					
Performance metrics	65.4	31.3	3.3	0.0	0.0	54.9	17.4	16.8
Access to third-party party provider's information systems	28.8	46.9	20.5	2.7	1.1	9.1	16.6	22.4
Joint review meetings	59.7	33.5	5.7	1.1	0.0	24.1	38.2	24.1
Customer satisfaction surveys	35.5	42.2	17.4	3.8	1.1	8.4	21.6	25.2
Audits by outside consultants	10.8	32.6	33.6	12.1	5.8	2.2	4.7	10.4

Figure 5.8 Effectiveness of monitoring methods. (*Source:* University of Maryland Supply Chain Management Center, *Logistics Outsourcing Survey, 1997.*)

The experiences of logistics executives interviewed show a strong preference for auditing and monitoring the outsourcing relationship through internal staff and joint committees with the third-party providers. Almost all of the company representatives interviewed highlighted the need for a partnership, not just a contractual relationship, with the third-party logistics provider. As the parts operations manager of a major European car manufacturer explained, "Maintaining a productive relationship involves good communication and a good setup whereby you have measures that have been agreed upon by both parties that are fair and representative of the goal that you are trying to complete. If you go into a situation where you have forced things upon a provider who feels he or she cannot deliver but takes it anyway, you are not going to have a long-term relationship." A logistics specialist from a worldwide manufacturer of computer equipment added: "We make sure that all of our third-party logistics providers increase productivity by at least 5 percent every year. We feel that is the only way to remain competitive. We hold third-party provider forums where we discuss how we can together be more productive. We believe that we should not just beat up the third-party logistics provider every year to provide lower costs. We want them to succeed. We do not want to eliminate their profit margins. We always try to work together toward productivity and encourage the third-party logistics provider to bring ideas to the table."

■ SUSTAINING A PRODUCTIVE RELATIONSHIP

Despite the potential benefits of outsourcing, the survey identified problem areas that may need special attention. One major concern was the learning curve associated with the initiation of a logistics service contract. As the logistics manager of a large computer company stated, "The third-party logistics provider has to thoroughly understand what our business is like. They need to learn it in depth and to learn it fast. For example, we ship a lot more in the last few weeks of the quarter than we do in the first few weeks. The third-party logistics provider said they have the flexibility to handle fluctuations in volume. But we certainly surprised them. All of a sudden, on the last day of the month, they could not handle our volume. We told them about this from the start, but they underestimated what it would be like. They got caught up in the averages, as opposed to looking at the actual business." In fact, a few interviewees mentioned that in functional areas with unique complexity and long learning curves (e.g., customer service), their companies have ruled out outsourcing as a matter of policy.

Another major issue was a third-party logistics provider being overloaded and unable to deliver on all their promises. As one interviewee put it, "These guys are operating so thin. Everyone wants to be a logistics provider. Companies change their sign and say they are now a logistics service provider. But they don't necessarily have the expertise they claim they have. For example, they told us they have all this great information technology. But we found out later through tours of other facilities we took that those IT systems were customer-owned information systems." Another interviewee noted that, "Third-party logistics providers make all sorts of claims about what their information systems can do. I say `show me'. It is such a critical issue for logistics. I cannot overemphasize this. If they cannot show you their systems, then they have to have an implementation plan as to when and how they are going to deliver on what they promise." This type of concern can only be addressed through a thorough and up-front review of a third-party logistics provider's systems and capabilities, or what one interviewee called "looking in the eyes" of the provider.

■ EVALUATING GAINS FROM LOGISTICS OUTSOURCING

The critical consideration for managers is the extent to which logistics outsourcing has served to benefit business operations. Survey results indicate that, in general, managers perceive that outsourcing has been a powerful contributor to their firms' competitive position (see Figure 5.9). This contribution is reflected both in an improvement in the firms' customer service levels (see Figure 5.10) and in a reduction of total logistics costs (see Figures 5.11 and 5.12). Figure 5.13 offers an overall summary of the total effects of logistics outsourcing on company operations.

➤ Competitive Advantage

The outsourced logistics functions seen as most effective in building competitive advantage include carrier selection and rate negotiation, fleet management, and shipment planning and consolidation. The emphasis in these functions is on flexibility in meeting both internal and external customer requirements. About 75 percent of respondents said the outsourcing of all supply-chain functions was somewhat or very effective in contributing to the company's competitive advantage.

The length of time a function has been outsourced does not appear to be directly related to its impact on competitive advantage. For example, the outsourced function rated as most effective in contributing to company competitive advantage was carrier selection/rate negotiation. This function had been outsourced by our respondents the least average number of years (4.4 years). The importance of having quality partnerships with a critical few carriers combined with the ability of major third-party logistics providers to

Functions	Very Effective	Somewhat Effective	Neither Effective nor Ineffective	Somewhat Ineffective	Very Ineffective	Number of Respondents
			(Percentage of Respondents)			
All supply-chain functions	33.3	47.6	14.3	2.4	2.4	42
Logistics information systems	30.1	51.8	13.3	2.4	2.4	83
Carrier selection and rate negotiation	51.5	39.6	4.0	2.0	3.0	101
Shipment planning	45.3	42.7	8.0	2.7	1.3	75
Fleet management	47.9	42.3	4.2	4.2	1.4	71
Warehousing and operations	42.4	41.6	12.0	2.4	1.6	125
Freight payments and auditing	42.3	33.5	16.9	5.2	2.0	248
Inventory management	25.8	35.5	29.0	9.7	0.0	31
Packaging	30.5	33.9	35.6	0.0	0.0	59
Order processing and fulfillment	45.2	35.7	14.3	4.8	0.0	42
Product returns	12.5	50.0	29.2	8.3	0.0	24

Figure 5.9 Effectiveness of outsourced functions in contributing to competitive advantage. (*Source:* University of Maryland Supply Chain Management Center, *Logistics Outsourcing Survey, 1997.*)

Functions	Very Effective	Somewhat Effective	Neither Effective nor Ineffective	Somewhat Ineffective	Very Ineffective	Number of Respondents
			(Percentage of Respondents)			
All supply-chain functions	32.5	37.5	25.0	5.0	0.0	40
Logistics information systems	38.8	41.3	11.3	5.0	3.8	80
Carrier selection and rate negotiation	34.7	37.8	19.4	5.1	3.1	98
Shipment planning	45.8	36.1	11.1	5.6	1.4	72
Fleet management	42.0	33.3	18.8	4.3	1.4	69
Warehousing and operations	35.2	43.4	16.4	4.1	0.8	122
Freight payments and auditing	22.2	26.7	38.3	8.6	3.7	220
Inventory management	32.3	25.8	32.3	9.7	0.0	31
Packaging	28.8	44.1	27.1	0.0	0.0	59
Order processing and fulfillment	42.9	33.3	19.0	4.8	0.0	42
Product returns	16.7	37.5	37.5	8.3	0.0	24

Figure 5.10 Effectiveness of outsourced functions in improving the company's customer service. (*Source:* University of Maryland Supply Chain Management Center, *Logistics Outsourcing Survey, 1997.*)

orchestrate these partnerships likely contributed to the high effectiveness rating for the carrier selection function.

➤ Customer Service

Three functions appear to contribute most to an improvement in a company's customer service performance: shipment planning and consolidation, order processing and fulfillment, and fleet management. The emphasis in these functions is on cutting delivery times and improving delivery accuracy to external customers. Figure 5.10 summarizes respondents' views on how effective outsourcing particular functions were at improving customer service.

➤ Cost Savings

The survey questionnaire focused both on the issue of how effective the outsourcing of various functions was at reducing logistics costs as well as on reductions in total logistics costs from the logistics outsourcing. Figure 5.11 provides the effectiveness results, while Figure 5.12 presents the estimates of total logistics cost savings experienced by respondents. Results show that the individual logistics functions generating the highest percentage of logistics cost savings are fleet management, carrier selection and rate negotiation, warehousing and operations, and freight payments and auditing. For these functions, the emphasis is on either rationalization of major fixed asset, or lowering variable costs through freight rate reductions or improved processes in handling payment and auditing of freight bills. The specific levels of logistics cost savings achieved during the first year for these functions are fleet management (10.5 percent), freight payments and audit-

Functions	Very Effective	Somewhat Effective	Neither Effective nor Ineffective	Somewhat Ineffective	Very Ineffective	Number of Respondents
			(Percentage of Respondents)			
All supply-chain functions	37.5	40.6	15.6	6.3	0.0	32
Logistics information systems	24.3	45.9	21.6	6.8	1.4	74
Carrier selection and rate negotiation	40.4	49.4	4.5	3.4	2.2	89
Shipment planning	35.9	46.9	12.5	4.7	0.0	64
Fleet management	43.8	43.8	7.8	4.7	0.0	64
Warehousing and operations	40.0	38.1	15.2	4.8	1.9	105
Freight payments and auditing	36.5	41.2	16.6	3.3	2.4	211
Inventory management	22.7	40.9	22.7	9.1	4.5	22
Packaging	24.5	46.9	26.5	2.0	0.0	49
Order processing and fulfillment	29.4	32.4	26.5	5.9	5.9	34
Product returns	5.6	44.4	38.9	5.6	5.6	18

Figure 5.11 Effectiveness of outsourced logistics functions in reducing total logistics costs. (*Source:* University of Maryland Supply Chain Management Center, *Logistics Outsourcing Survey, 1997.*)

Functions	Year 1		Years 2, 3, and 4	
	Average Savings (%)	Standard Deviation (%)	Average Savings (%)	Standard Deviation (%)
All supply-chain functions	21.3	17.3	15.1	14.2
Logistics information systems	7.3	10.1	6.0	5.0
Carrier selection and rate negotiation	10.2	9.2	7.7	7.6
Shipment planning	5.7	8.5	5.4	11.3
Fleet management	10.5	10.2	6.8	5.0
Warehousing and operations	9.5	8.4	8.4	8.5
Freight payments and auditing	10.5	13.8	9.4	12.6
Inventory management	3.5	1.9	5.0	3.6
Packaging	8.8	13.7	8.5	12.7
Order processing and fulfillment	2.5	11.2	4.5	13.8
Product returns	2.1	2.7	3.1	2.6

Figure 5.12 Total logistics cost savings from outsourced logistics functions. (*Source:* University of Maryland Supply Chain Management Center, *Logistics Outsourcing Survey, 1997.*)

ing (10.5 percent), and carrier selection and rate negotiations (10.2 percent).

In addition, the savings from outsourcing appear to be significantly greater and more sustained from a strategic approach to total supply-chain outsourcing than from only outsourcing individual functions. Survey respondents indicated that the first year logistics cost savings from total supply-chain outsourcing averaged 21.3 percent with additional annual savings of 15.1 percent in years two, three, and four. However, as companies gradually outsource a larger number of individual functions, the marginal annual savings obtained per function decreases. This decline may be the result of a lack of integration resulting from an improvised outsourcing policy.

Overall, firms indicate that annual logistics cost savings from outsourcing in years 2, 3, and 4 are less than they are in year 1. For many functions the fall-off is between 20 percent and 30 percent. However, order processing and fulfillment and product returns are exceptions to this pattern, showing annual savings in years 2, 3, and 4 that exceed those of year 1.

➤ Innovation

The ability of a third-party logistics provider to bring new perspectives and a more holistic vision of supply-chain management is another benefit companies experienced. As one executive in a major computer firm expressed it, "The best thing third-party logistics providers could bring to the table would be innovation and change, rather than just optimizing the current situation. I'd ask them what they will do to change the way we do business that creates competitive advantage for us."

The radical rethinking of supply-chain activities and the integration of third-party logistics capabilities into process reengineering can have significant positive effects. The logistics manager at a major manufacturer described his company's transformation:

> Since 1992, the company has doubled in size while the outbound logistics costs as a percentage of sales are less than half of what they used to be in 1992 and the total dollars we spend on outbound logistics is less today than in 1992. We radically redesigned our process. We had to eliminate 10 warehouses worldwide. We had to shut down all our factory warehouses. We had to let go of 700 people. Today, we have one worldwide logistics

organization and a single director of logistics. We took those 700 people out of the process and put in a third-party logistics provider. We eliminated warehouses in our regions. If there are warehouses, those are very small and owned by a third-party logistics provider.

➤ Information Technology

One level of change that the third-party logistics provider can bring is information technology (IT), which is clearly growing in importance. IT systems for total supply-chain management, shipment tracking and in-transit visibility, and inventory management and continual replenishment are becoming crucial in attaining competitive advantage. This point came out in various interviews as the need to "leverage the technology of third-party logistics providers" and "to get the third-party logistics firm to provide the information systems platform." This sentiment appeared to represent a desire to avoid steep sunk costs in the fast-moving technology arena by passing those costs onto third-party logistics providers.

➤ Overall Effects

Outsourcing the following functions is most likely to lead to competitive advantage: carrier rate selection and rate negotiation, fleet management, and shipment planning (see Figure 5.13). These functions emphasize flexibility in meeting both internal and external customer requirements. The most effective logistics functions to outsource in order to improve customer service are: shipment planning, order processing, and fleet management. With these functions, the emphasis is on cutting delivery times and improving delivery accuracy to external customers. Fleet management, carrier selection and rate negotiation, and warehousing and operations are the most effective functions to outsource for lowering total logistics costs. The emphasis in these functions is on major fixed asset rationalization (i.e., warehousing and operations and fleet management) and on lowering variable costs through rate reduction (i.e., carrier rate selection and negotiation).

The results in Figure 5.13 reflect averages, and, as always, some respondents are on either side of the average. For example, a few firms reported no cost savings from logistics outsourcing; indeed, several had cost increases due to poor experiences with outsourcing providers. Another caveat: High average cost savings may reflect high

Building Competitive Advantage	Improving Customer Service	Lowering Total Logistics Costs
➤ Carrier selection and rate negotiation	➤ Shipment planning and consolidation	➤ Fleet management
➤ Fleet management	➤ Order processing and fulfillment	➤ Carrier selection and rate negotiation
➤ Shipment planning	➤ Fleet management	➤ Warehousing and operations
Emphasis is on:	*Emphasis is on:*	*Emphasis is on:*
➤ Flexibility in meeting both internal and external customer requirements	➤ Cutting delivery times and improving delivery accuracy to external customers	➤ Major fixed assets rationalization
		➤ Reducing variable costs through rate reduction

Figure 5.13 Most effective outsourced functions by result.

levels of logistics inefficiency prior to outsourcing. If firms have already made some improvements in logistics systems, the level of improvements expected from outsourcing may need to be modified.

Furthermore, additional analysis of the survey results indicates that structural characteristics of firms and industries influence the cost effectiveness of logistics outsourcing. Firms with annual sales above $500 million had significantly lower annual cost savings from outsourcing than firms with $500 million or less in annual sales. It could very well be that the smaller firms have greater inefficiencies in their logistics activities prior to the initiation of outsourcing activity and thus experience greater savings. On the other hand, third party firms may offer economies of scale that the smaller firms themselves cannot realize.

One final point—we found that cost savings benefits are significantly higher for companies participating in mature markets, whose final products have the following characteristics: low value, low technical complexity, long replacement cycles, and low levels of after-sale service. However, in the long run, this advantage is likely to diminish.

■ BEST PRACTICES IN LOGISTICS OUTSOURCING MANAGEMENT

Survey responses highlighted a number of best practices in managing tasks related to outsourcing logistics services. These include:

➤ Establishing core internal management strength in logistics for effective evaluation of internal and outsourced logistics processes and costs

➤ Establishing the costs of outsourcing and comparing them with insourcing costs

➤ Recognizing the differences in planning requirements for outsourcing different logistics functions

➤ For maximum cost savings, taking a strategic
approach to total outsourcing

➤ Using metrics extensively in monitoring the outsourcing partner

➤ Establishing regular meetings and defining lines of
communications with outsourcing partners to cement
the relationship

➤ Building continuous improvement into the relationship to overcome drawbacks of outsourcing

These best practices are discussed below.

*Establish core internal management strength in logistics for
effective management of outsourced logistics services.* Establishing core internal management capabilities is critical for
evaluation of the logistics systems/supply chain. These
capabilities include the ability to:

➤ Map logistics processes and costs

➤ Identify third-party logistics providers

➤ Generate bids from providers

➤ Conduct cost benefit analyses on proposals to determine whether to insource/outsource

➤ Establish contractual arrangements

➤ Monitor performance

Thus, creating empowered core internal leadership with
a commitment to and expertise in logistics is the first step in
creating a coherent logistics system. Without this leadership
in place, all future actions to assess and improve the logistics system will be suboptimal, including the decision to
outsource. Internal leadership is critical in mapping logis-

tics processes and costs in order to understand the cost and benefits of in sourcing versus outsourcing. If the decision is made to outsource one or more logistics functions, a chief logistics officer (CLO) is best qualified to manage the company's relationship with the third-party provider.

Establish costs of outsourcing and compare with those of insourcing. While logistics outsourcing may be an effective solution to a company's efforts to improve logistics processes and costs, the potential for savings may be inversely related to the current system's level of efficiency. Indeed, the highest percentage cost reductions will occur in companies whose logistics systems were most inefficient prior to outsourcing. Because insourcing can also be effective, comparing and contrasting internally generated versus externally generated bids to manage logistics functions can stimulate competition and spur internal improvements.

Recognize the differences in planning requirements for outsourcing different logistics functions. Companies have longer experience with outsourcing more routine functions. The more recently outsourced functions are those that are more planning intensive and require dynamic modeling to determine optimal configurations and expected cost savings. For example, outsourcing warehouse functions involves increasingly more sophisticated procedures, the development of automation systems, and a desire to focus on core competencies. As a result, the time horizon to outsource these planning-intensive functions may be longer than the horizon for the more routine functions.

For maximum cost savings, take a strategic approach to total outsourcing. Companies take three approaches to outsourcing logistics functions:

➤ Outsourcing one function at a time

➤ Outsourcing two or more functions initially and then "leaping" to total supply-chain management to try to achieve higher system gains

➤ Outsourcing the whole supply chain from the outset to seek maximum gains from system synergy

Outsourced functions rated as most effective in building competitive advantage are the ones that emphasize flexibility in meeting both the internal and external customer requirements. However, to improve customer service, it is most effective to outsource functions that cut delivery times and improve delivery accuracy to external customers. The top savings-generating functions emphasize either the rationalization of a major fixed asset or lowering of variable costs through freight rate reductions or improved processes in handling payments and auditing of freight bills. However, strong indications suggest that savings from outsourcing are significantly greater and more sustained from a strategic approach to total supply-chain outsourcing.

Use metrics extensively in monitoring the outsourcing partner. Survey respondents ranked metrics as the most effective tool in monitoring the performance of third-party logistics providers. Metrics are also more useful in measuring customer satisfaction with outsourced logistics services than customer satisfaction surveys. Lean core logistics capabilities and extensive performance-monitoring metrics enable an organization to gain strategic control over a dispersed network of operating sites and supplier/distribution partners.

Establish regular meetings and defined lines of communications with outsourcing partners to cement the relationship. Nearly two of three survey respondents considered joint review meetings a very effective way to evaluate third-party logistics providers' performance. Regular interactions between knowledgeable in-house staff and the staff of the third-party logistics providers helps establish productive relationships, an environment of trust, and common business objectives. One interviewee recommended that the relationship between a company and a third-party logistics provider begin with frequent formal meetings to uncover issues and problems immediately. Without these meetings, the new partnership can flounder.

Build in continuous improvement. In general, companies outsourcing logistics functions realize early gains, but the question is for how long will these gains be sustainable. Companies need to build into the outsourcing relationship methods to achieve continuous improvements. For example, a major computer and electronics manufacturer has built into its third-party logistics contract clauses to sustain gains over an extended period. The contract requires the third-party logistics provider to generate five identifiable proposals per year for improvement and implement one of these proposals each year. Overall, the contract requires that the provider reduce total logistics costs by 10 percent per year.

■ REAPING THE REWARDS

Companies that actively manage their relationships with third-party logistics service providers and adopt some or all of the best practices outlined in this chapter will reap the biggest rewards from supply-chain outsourcing. These rewards can translate into substantial reductions in cost, significant gains in productivity, accelerated speed to market, and overall superiority in supply-chain competitiveness.

Reaping such rewards, while tantalizing, is not an easy task. It requires considerable time and hard work. In the next chapter, we examine the first and most important step toward achieving supply-chain superiority—the self assessment. We present a detailed process for analyzing exactly where your logistics/supply-chain operations are on the performance scale. We provide an easy-to-use tool for evaluating your current operations and pinpointing areas of poor performance, high cost, or unnecessary redundancies.

Part II

Applying Best Practices to Your Company

Chapter

Assessing and Improving Your Supply Chain: A Self-Diagnostic Process

Chapters 5 through 7 contain a tool kit for logistics and supply-chain managers who want to design and implement their own unique extended-enterprise model. This chapter contains an integrated data-gathering methodology to help you assess the current state or *baseline* of your supply chain. This self-assessment is the first step in developing a new and improved supply chain in the extended-enterprise model. This chapter also contains a methodology that can help you use the best practices described in earlier chapters to move, in a logical progression, from your baseline to an extended-enterprise model. Chapter 7 presents a supply-chain diagnostic template to help you visualize your material and information flows. It also integrates assessment activities into the enterprise development process and shows the linkages between supply-chain functions at each stage in the process. The two chapters are designed to work, and be used, together.

The basic rationale underlying this tool kit is the concept that supply-chain management is a central enabler of the extended enterprise. Thus, logistics and supply-chain managers are well placed to help their organizations create the integrated relationships that underpin an effective extended enterprise and its competitive advantages.

■ WHY ESTABLISH A BASELINE?

Fully completing the assessment process outlined below will give managers a baseline from which to develop benchmarks—the key tool successful companies use to synchronize supply-chain elements and create productivity improvement opportunities. Benchmarking means comparing your logistics operation performance levels against those of performance leaders in diverse industries. It helps companies develop the skills and knowledge needed to fuel productivity improvements and create competitive advantages based on either being the low-cost provider, or positioning the company as a unique market leader.[1] A complete understanding of your logistics/supply-chain structure and processes—as well as sound data on your own baseline performance—is an absolute prerequisite to making valid comparisons with industry leaders. Such knowledge also forms the basis for any future documentation of the effects of new integration strategies and other supply-chain process changes.

➤ Extended Enterprise Methodology

In completing the self-assessment process outlined below, it is important to have an overview of all phases of extended-enterprise development. Based on our survey research about

Phase 1— Baselining	Phase 2— Benchmarking	Phase 3— Best Practices Development
➤ Establishing the organization's current state of logistics strategies, systems, and operating performance levels.	➤ Comparing the organization's strategies, systems, and operating performance levels with direct industry competitors or with best-in-class organizations outside the industry.	➤ Analyzing logistics options to determine the most efficient and effective implementation pathways to close the previously identified gaps and meet future needs.
➤ Mapping the physical distribution network and the flow of materials between supply, production, and distribution points in the network.	➤ Defining the gap between current organizational strategies/systems/operating performance levels and current best practices.	➤ Repositioning internal assets, using new practices and technologies to reach higher performance levels.
➤ Mapping information systems and flows that correspond to transactions in the physical distribution network.	➤ Assessing trend lines and anticipated changes in best practices in order to develop relevant supply-chain design guidelines and operating performance requirements.	➤ Selecting and recruiting external/outsourced assets.
➤ Profiling management practices, (e.g., carrier/supplier management practices).		➤ Developing an action plan for high-level integration of internal and external assets.

Figure 6.1 Overview of a three-phased extended enterprise methodology.

how corporations sequence the transformation process, we have defined a methodology for building a truly extended enterprise. Baselining and benchmarking are the first two phases comprising this methodology, which is described in

Figure 6.1. The third phase features the actual implementation of best practices and supply-chain integration.

We must emphasize that this process varies in its time and resource commitments, depending on a firm's characteristics, competitive position, and commitment of senior management. We know some firms that have accomplished all three phases in 18 months, while for others it is an ongoing process.

The rest of this chapter describes the self-assessment process that takes place in phase 1. It will produce the baseline you need to move on to the other two phases of extended enterprise development.

■ THE SUPPLY-CHAIN DIAGNOSTIC: AN OVERVIEW

The Supply-Chain Diagnostic is a comprehensive survey instrument that begins with an assessment of a firm's overall orientation/understanding of supply-chain issues and ends with information on the efficiency of current supply-chain processes. This overview section contains a short description of each of the diagnostic's four parts, including:

1. Overall direction and orientation

2. Supply-chain products/information flows

3. Operations assessment for each core product

4. Supply-chain management practices

Subsequent sections provide a more detailed discussion of each of these parts. That discussion will highlight the motivation behind the assessment questions included and will explain how you can use the information you collect to move forward in crafting a highly tuned extended enterprise. It also will suggest important issues to consider in assessing each area.

The primary objective of assessing "Overall Direction and Orientation" (Part 1) is to determine the firm's existing state of knowledge about its overall logistics/supply-chain situation. This initial task forces logistics/supply-chain executives to define their understanding of performance problems and symptoms, including perceptions about the underlying factors and root causes creating these problems. While the symptoms are typically located within specific logistics functions, the underlying problems and root causes often span multiple functional areas. Supply-chain problems are generally embedded in multifunctional tasks, while their causes often reside in structural elements of the supply chain. This part of the diagnostic, therefore, is designed to alert managers to problems requiring cross-functional solutions. It will be important to review your responses to this part of the diagnostic in light of what you learn in the other sections.

The "Supply-Chain Products/Information Flows" element (Part 2) of the diagnostic is a mapping exercise that enables a holistic view of the supply chain. It involves identifying and tracking each of the handoffs involved in moving both physical products and information through the chain, and placing those handoffs in the context of the overall supply chain and its competitive environment. Understanding and flowcharting supply-chain activities is a critical prerequisite to streamlining and integrating them.

Part 3 delves deeper into the nitty-gritty of the existing supply chain, using an "Operations Assessment" process for each of the firm's core products. This Operations Assessment is the tool used to compile detailed product flow and cost information at each stage of the supply chain. The information-collection process for each product starts at the customer level and moves backward in the chain to suppliers.

Finally, Part 4, "Supply-Chain Management Practices," focuses on identifying the entities in charge of planning, organizing, operating, monitoring, and controlling all the internal logistics functional areas in the supply chain. Mapping these responsibilities clearly helps a company identify management weaknesses, disconnects, redundancies, and the like.

This process also can be applied to relationships with external suppliers of both products (e.g., raw materials) and services (e.g., transportation). This tool helps a company assess these external relationships, allowing management to get a fix on how well these relationships work and where their shortcomings lie. Thus, it allows a company to establish the base point for any supplier relationship-improvement efforts.

➤ Part 1: Overall Direction and Orientation

The first step in establishing directions for performance improvement throughout the extended enterprise is to clearly identify the supply chain's most evident symptoms of poor performance. These symptoms reflect ineffective use of tangible and intangible resources in multiple logistics functions. For example, in transportation, symptoms of poor performance show up in unacceptable levels of shipment damage, high frequency of missed delivery dates, or extensive use of premium transportation modes. In inventory operations, poor performance symptoms include excessive safety stocks, low annual inventory-turnover ratios, or high material handling costs. Finally, in customer service operations, poor performance symptoms include low order fill rates, long cycle times, or excessive lost-sale costs.

The second step in establishing directions for performance improvement involves identifying the underlying problems causing the symptoms. Generally, this effort focuses on specific supply-chain tasks within or across logistics functional areas. This step is a prerequisite for defining *common performance linkages* (i.e., cause and effect relationships) throughout the supply chain. For instance, extensive use of premium transportation results from poor planning and coordination between manufacturing and outbound logistics activities. Such poor planning eats up valuable order cycle time, forcing the company to use high-cost transportation in order to meet customer service commitments. With inventory, a low turnover ratio may derive from poor forecasting ability, which, in turn, leads to manufacturing and stocking low-demand/high-value units.

The third step in establishing directions for performance improvement involves identifying the root causes of underlying problems. Root causes often originate from the physical architecture of the supply chain, and their effects cascade throughout the organization. For example, distribution centers may be located too far from major points of sale. This network design deficiency causes excessive delivery lead times that, in turn, unnecessarily complicate the task of planning deliveries. This planning problem, in turn, manifests itself in multiple symptoms of poor performance (e.g., excessive use of premium transportation, low order fill rates, and excessive safety stocks).

In other circumstances, the manner in which information, skills, and expertise are organized throughout the supply chain can be the root cause for a different constellation of problems. For example, a disconnect in the information flow resulting from poor coordination between customer service/order fulfillment and manufacturing may be a root cause of poor forecasting. Poor forecasting, in turn, contributes to manufacturing and stocking the wrong products at the wrong time. This forecasting problem will, in the end, play out in low inventory-turnover ratios across the product line.

Finally, the overall orientation assessment must include clearly defining the firm's competitive environment and its impact on logistics performance. Technological, social, economic, and regulatory factors all have significant effects, not only on how you map the interaction of supply-chain symptoms, problems, and causes, but also on how you prioritize improvement actions.

➤ Part 2: Supply-Chain Products/Information Flows

The mapping of high-level flows of both information and goods for all the firm's major products throughout the supply chain requires identifying the following:

1. Each party in the extended enterprise

2. Their physical locations

3. The handoffs that occur between and among them

In general, participating parties include suppliers, manufacturers, distributors, sellers, and customers. These entities usually have multiple locations from which and to which different flows of goods and information are moved. The map should include each of these locations, their material flow handoffs, and their related technological tools such as information systems, warehousing equipment, and transportation assets.

Flow mapping facilitates the process of identifying supply-chain performance symptoms, problems, and causes. It creates a visual representation or diagram of the extended enterprise's operations, helping to pinpoint bottlenecks where information and material flow inefficiently. For example, centralized product inventories are a common bottleneck. While centralizing inventories may help improve fill rates by reducing variability across distribution centers, it can cause high material handling and transportation costs. The supply-chain flow map will highlight the need to evaluate this tradeoff.

Flow maps also help identify opportunities to improve efficiency through economies of scale, scope, and coordination. One way to achieve supply-chain economy of scale and scope is by consolidating material flows across multiple extended-enterprise partners. For example, by consolidating loads from multiple suppliers or distribution centers located near each other, firms can realize full truckload economies. Consolidating information flows throughout different stages of the supply chain and across multiple extended-enterprise partners can create supply-chain economies of coordination. Specifically, these economies result from multiple supply-chain events and transactions (e.g., customer ordering, freight payments, and shipment planning) occurring at a single time and location. A single entity can dynamically process customer orders and plan, track, and bill freight shipments more effectively than could multiple entities with dissimilar skills and incompatible information systems.

➤ Part 3: Operations Assessment for Each Core Product

It is important to substantiate the validity of problems/ causes and opportunities for improvement identified in the first two parts of the diagnostic before taking action on them. Gathering detailed data on operations and managerial practices throughout the extended enterprise, using Part 3 of the diagnostic tool, can provide this confirmation. The resulting information also helps ensure that a change to correct a root cause will not negatively impact other areas of the supply chain. In addition, complete data are needed to measure supply-chain performance with regard to its various activity interdependencies. This section addresses data-collection needs in six key areas:

1. Customer demand

2. Demand forecasting

3. Inventory management

4. Manufacturing performance and processes

5. Supplier management performance and processes

6. Supply-chain management practices

It provides the foundation for an integrated analysis of your findings.

Customer Demand

The operational assessment of each of the firm's core products involves reviewing how the relationships among extended enterprise partners are planned, configured, operated, and controlled. This review starts with information about the factors that directly influence patterns of customer demand. It is essential to gather the most basic information about the number and size of customers and their demand patterns. This information will give an initial demand profile product-by-product, pointing up variations and anomalies.

In conjunction with customer demand information, it is important to recognize that product demand is influenced by exogenous factors. Identifying and measuring these factors to the extent possible will help you find firms with similar situations when you begin the benchmarking process. Relevant exogenous factors include general business conditions and the state of the economy, competitor actions and reactions, government legislative actions, marketplace trends such as product life cycles and changes in styles and fashion, and technological innovations.

Demand Forecasting

Having characterized the basic customer demand factors, it is important to understand the methods and procedures used to process that information as part of the overall forecasting process. To accomplish this, the logistics/supply-chain manager should review current customer demand management processes. Specifically, it is important to:

➤ Determine the methods involved in replenishing final products at each point of sale

➤ Understand how the firm gets access to information about customer purchasing patterns for its forecasts

➤ Find out what technologies facilitate interaction with customers

➤ Understand the processes used to track and measure customer service

This information will be important in subsequent benchmarking efforts.

Inventory Management

The operational assessment also should include an evaluation of inventory management performance and processes. In general terms, the management of inventories must contribute to profit by servicing the marketing and financial needs of the firm. The goal is not to make all items available at all times since this may be detrimental to the profitability of all the partners in the extended enterprise. Instead, it is to meet the required demand at a minimum cost.

To establish the extended enterprise's competitive position, it is important to translate operational activities into specific performance terms. Although each firm is different, in general, inventory management functions support business activities by optimizing three elements: customer service, inventory costs, and operating costs. For maximum utility, baselining and benchmarking efforts must address all three performance targets simultaneously.

To measure customer service, metrics may capture factors such as stockout costs in order to understand the "availability of stock" to customers. Customer service metrics should also integrate measures of fulfillment reliability and delivery performance. We recommend that these measures be segregated according to the origin/destination lanes established in the overall mapping process. To measure inventory costs, you must consider metrics establishing the financial resources tied up in inventory, rather than simply considering the number of product units stocked. Operating cost metrics must include the costs involved in warehouse operations, that is material handling, packaging, leasing costs, insurance costs, obsolescence and damage costs, and the costs associated with distributing the products to customers. We recommend that you also segregate these costs by origin/destination lanes and transportation modes. Further, the percentage of annual shipping volumes should be assigned to the corresponding shipping lanes to verify unbalanced cost conditions.

Once you establish the inventory-management performance baseline, the next task is to evaluate how the existing combinations of resources contribute to the present level of performance. Such resources can be combined to include physical and capital assets, human skills, and corporate knowledge. For example, one such combination involves using distribution warehouses to consolidate, repackage, and redistribute final products, work in progress, and raw materials. Identifying resources currently used in implementing this combination technique will be important during the benchmarking processes outlined in Chapter 7. Such knowledge forms the basis for any future supply-chain rationalization.

Manufacturing Performance and Processes

The operational assessment should also include an evaluation of manufacturing performance and processes. In general terms, the assessment of manufacturing performance should center on production's contribution to corporate profits. That is, to what extent production keeps costs down and achieves the high levels of quality and product differentiation that translate into higher revenues. To evaluate this aspect of performance, firms must measure how responsive their production capabilities are to the changing competitive conditions identified earlier in this baselining process. Marketplace conditions create more and more pressure on production capabilities to be nimble, accommodate rapid product design changes, and respond to swings in demand volume, all the while manufacturing products with consistently high quality.

Furthermore, companies must track the extent to which they can reduce the costs associated with manufacturing and distribution to warehouses. To this end, you need to establish the extent to which manufacturing activities consume resources (i.e., physical and financial assets, human resources, and corporate expertise) but do not create product value (reflected in the revenue stream of the extended enterprise). Similarly, businesses must also identify imbalances in costs and value-adding streams associated with distributing goods to warehouses and customers. You can do this by segregating origin/destination lanes, transportation modes, and the percentage of annual shipping volumes assigned to the corresponding shipping lanes.

As before, once the manufacturing performance baseline is established, it is necessary to evaluate the resource combination techniques that currently make up the company's cost structures and value creation. One combination technique involves using both standardized and customized processes to balance high customer-order fill rates against variability in demand. As with inventory management, the resources needed to implement the standardized and customized processes can be benchmarked and thus are important to identify. Overall, the extent to which physical, human, and knowledge resources are committed to achieve optimal customer-order fill rates and low variability of manufacturing operations must also become part of the manufacturing-resource baseline used in subsequent benchmarking efforts.

Supplier Management Performance and Processes

The final step in the operational assessment for each product is an evaluation of supplier management performance and processes. The goal of any supplier management program is to balance three distinct firm needs: lowest parts cost, timely parts availability, and high product quality. Thus baselining (and, eventually benchmarking) must simultaneously address all three performance targets.

The first target deals with price paid, and is clearly a critical component of a baselining effort. The cost of product received from suppliers includes its attendant distribution costs. We recommend segmenting these costs by origin/destination lanes and by transportation mode. Furthermore, we advise assigning the percentage of annual shipping volumes to each of the identified shipping lanes in order to verify unbalanced cost conditions.

To evaluate suppliers' performance on meeting your service requirements, you must have good data on order-to-delivery cycles for parts, delivery performance, and, of course, product quality (i.e., number of defects). Assessing performance on both of these targets requires detailed information on the number and geographic location of all the suppliers used in the manufacturing process of each product.

Once again, the assessment should include evaluating the ways in which resources are combined to create the observed levels of performance. In the case of supplier management, resources (physical and capital assets, human skills, and corporate knowledge) are combined in multiple ways, each capable of being benchmarked. One technique involves limiting the number of parts-suppliers used to achieve volume-purchase discounts as well as to reduce transaction costs (as a result of dealing with fewer individual suppliers).

A second technique is exploring the use of new technology in searching for and ordering parts. Some firms are turning over their supplier management activities to third parties, capable of searching for and ordering parts on the Internet from prequalified suppliers. With a reliable baseline, these practices can also be benchmarked.

➤ Part 4: Supply-Chain Management Practices

The baselining process concludes with identifying current supply-chain management practices used throughout the extended enterprise. As discussed in Chapter 2, effective management involves two sets of responsibilities, both of which should be objectively assessed. The first is the internal *planning, operation, and control of activities needed to coordinate and synchronize flows of goods and information across logistics functions* such as inventory management, transportation management, and materials management. The second is the *management of relationships among supply-chain participants* such as carriers and suppliers.

Baselining *managerial practices within the internal, core firm* focuses on how corporate responsibility lines are drawn within the organization structure, and on identifying the organizational framework that houses them. This assessment should identify the entities in charge of planning, operating, monitoring, and controlling all of the core firm's routine supply-chain management/logistics functions. To this end, you need to determine which area of the organization (i.e., point-of-sale sites, manufacturing plants, strategic business units, or headquarters) is in charge of devising policies and guidelines used in planning supply-chain activities. Important activities to consider are the planning and management of finished goods, work in process, and raw material inventories, shipments, and the distribution center's and warehouse's configurations and locations. Furthermore, it is essential to establish what areas of the organization control the daily logistics operations of the core of the extended enterprise. Important operational functions to consider are outbound and inbound transportation, carrier and transportation mode selection, freight payments, material handling, product packaging, and order processing.

Chapter 2 discussed the importance of applying best practices to manage the relationship among supply-chain participants. In fact, firms can use these same best practices as the yardstick with which they baseline their own practices. With specific regard to carriers, the baseline assessment should include an analysis of ways in which the firm interacts with these vital service providers. Specifically, analysis should:

➤ Determine which contracting methodologies are used to regulate, measure, and control multiyear partnerships with carriers.

➤ Identify current methodologies used to aggregate inbound and outbound shipment volumes.

➤ Explore current processes used to assign transportation liabilities for transportation freight.

➤ Determine to the extent to which freight bills are audited and how frequently this process is performed.

➤ Establish the level and characteristics of electronic data interchange (EDI) for shipment invoicing/payment and attaining in-transit visibility of goods.

We also recommend that the baselining assessment include an analysis of ways in which the firm interacts routinely with its suppliers, particularly as regards the use of electronic tools for supplier management. Electronic tools include online requests for quotations; electronic catalogues to display supplier products in a standard format for internal employee purchasing; and EDI systems for purchase orders, advance-shipping notices, and invoice payment. The assessment also should consider methods for creating long-term relationships with suppliers, including mechanisms such as corporatewide purchasing agreements and quality partnerships with core suppliers—and systems for measuring performance in these relationships.

■ MANAGING AN EFFECTIVE ASSESSMENT PROCESS

Managers should realize that these data-gathering activities are extensive, requiring significant resources and time commitment to accomplish. Some firms may lack the most fundamental data for baselining product and information flows, much less costs. Consequently, it is critical to involve a broad cross section of the firm's functional areas, as well as external suppliers and customers. Finally, the assessment project must have the commitment and support of senior management. Without that, major self-assessments like that described in this chapter will flounder.

While the self-assessment diagnostic contained here and in the next chapter contains research-based guidelines for developing an extended enterprise, each business unit using the process will have unique considerations. Industry conditions vary widely and generate their own unique opportunities and threats. Because of that, they necessitate distinct internal competencies and relationships with enterprise partners. For example, computer manufacturers operate on very small margins in a lightening-fast, volatile consumer market. Given the slimness of their margins, these companies place a premium on extended-enterprise design that minimizes inventory and maximizes customization of finished products for the consumer. By contrast, chemical industry firms operate under tremendous regulatory and civil liability burdens. These companies place a premium on extended-enterprise design that maximizes strategic control of risk and seeks to ensure safe and reliable practices of all supply-chain partners.

In addition to differences across industries, the design of an extended enterprise must also take into account differences based on the size of the firm. The size of the company in relation to its competitors significantly defines the nature of the strategic actions taken to maximize internal resources. For example, upstart firms can combine their own resources and those of their supply-chain partners to seize new opportunities and reap entrepreneurial profit. These partnerships can exploit competitive uncertainty and market niches overlooked by more traditional firms. On the other hand, larger firms with market power and leadership can use their formidable internal resources and those of their supply-chain partners to saturate markets and meet large-scale customer demand.

Despite these differences, all firms today must find new ways to integrate their enterprisewide logistics activities and marry the demands of their competitive environment with strategies and supply-chain structures. As business evolves from head-to-head competition between individual firms, to competition between supply chains, the success of any extended enterprise will hinge on how well it synchronizes these components—environment, strategy and structure. The diagnostic described in this chapter and the template that follows in Chapter 7 can help you create the information base needed to achieve this synchronization.

Chapter

7

Benchmarking for Better Results

David Kearns, the former CEO of Xerox, defined benchmarking as "the continuous process of measuring product, services, and practices against the toughest competitors, or those companies recognized as industry leaders."[1] Comparing performance in this way is vital to a company's strategic vision and competitive positioning. It enables leaders to see the potential for breakthrough gains and adapt the best practices that helped other companies achieve high performance.

Previous chapters provided guidance and tools for the first phase in the benchmarking process: collecting the data to understand current performance, performance problems, and the root causes of those problems. This chapter shows you how to use that information. First, it describes a five-step benchmarking process. Then it presents a case study example that illustrates how to use the benchmarking process to direct performance improvement efforts and adopt relevant best practices.

■ WHAT TO BENCHMARK

Firms can compare their supply-chain performance with best practices at the performance metric, process, and strategic levels. At the first level, you can compare metrics, such as inventory turnover and fill rates, against the metrics of best practices firms in their industry or another industry. At the next level, you can benchmark specific processes in functional areas, such as inventory management or production. At this level, you need not choose direct competitors to benchmark; you can choose firms identified as good performers in the focal processes.

The useful aim of both performance metric and process benchmarking is incremental performance improvement. At the highest level, however, firms can engage in strategic benchmarking by comparing several functional areas and divisions to other firms. The objective here is to realize major changes in higher-level processes. At this level, for example, a firm might compare its market positioning to best practices firms in the industry.

In addition to benchmarking against other firms (external benchmarking), you can also conduct internal benchmarking—comparing various divisions or units within a firm.

■ THE BENCHMARKING PROCESS

The key steps in the benchmarking process appear below. Firms can use them to benchmark externally at both the process and strategic levels.

> *Step 1: Collect and analyze baseline data using an appropriate diagnostic tool,* such as the self-diagnostic tool featured in Chapter 6 and the Appendix. Focus data-gathering particularly on functions in which the

company shows *symptoms* of underperforming. Then, identify the *problems* underlying the symptoms and their *root causes,* which may cut across multiple areas of the supply chain.

Step 2: Identify and gather data on best practice companies including competitors and/or high performers in any industry. Focus data collection on the processes or strategies related to the root causes of your performance problems. Obtain data comparable to your baseline information.

Step 3: Identify and analyze performance gaps between your baseline data and the data you gathered on benchmark firms.

Step 4: Develop a plan to reengineer your processes to close performance gaps. Considerations in developing this plan include:

➤ *Prioritizing actions to improve performance.* Typically, the benchmarking process will reveal several performance gaps that need to be closed. A firm must determine which process to reengineer first, which second, and so forth. A possible way to prioritize actions would be to use financial techniques, such as net present value calculations, payback periods, or cost/benefit analysis, to rank-order the reengineering initiatives.

➤ *Obtaining the buy-in of top management.* Top management is often looking for quick returns on investment. Therefore, it may be best to undertake those reengineering initiatives that are expected to provide large cost reductions or revenue improvements within the first year of implementation, even if long-term benefits from other initiatives are higher.

➤ *Considering potential synergies or diseconomies among reengineering initiatives.* Due consideration must be given to how a reengineering effort affects other departments within the organization and other firms within the supply chain, as well as other reengineering initiatives. It may be, for example, that production reengineering can save considerable money within the production department, but will result in additional warehousing, transportation, or supply costs.

➤ *Focusing on the overall competitive position of the firm.* It is important to assess the impact of the reengineering initiative on the current and future competitive positions of the firm. For example, reengineering efforts that emphasize cost cutting over improved customer service may conflict with an overall corporate strategy of being the service leader in the industry.

➤ *Making insourcing/outsourcing decisions.* In reengineering a process to close a performance gap, a company must determine whether it intends to manage the reengineered process internally or externally. As outlined previously, this decision will depend on whether the process is part of the firm's core competencies, the relative costs of insourcing and outsourcing, and whether the firm has the resources, including technology, to manage the process in-house.

Step 5: Implement the reengineering plan. The actual implementation process will vary considerably between firms. However, common considerations include identifying a champion to guide the implementation process, determining the timing of the implementation, training managers, operations staff, and clerical personnel in new procedures, and deciding whether to include outside consultants in the implementation process.

■ USING THE BENCHMARKING PROCESS: A CASE EXAMPLE

In this section of the chapter, we provide a case example of the benchmarking process. This example is based on a composite profile of firms for which the authors of this book have consulted. The case company is a large (10,000 plus employees), multiproduct, multidivisional firm with a high-technology focus. The firm has been formed through a series of acquisitions and mergers. The fact that the firm is large and multidivisional means that integration across divisions and functions is important. The high-technology focus implies that markets are highly volatile and, as such, place a premium on demand forecasting, demand management, and flexible production. Because the firm was formed through a series of acquisitions and mergers, differences between divisions are likely in areas such as corporate culture, information technology, and supplier bases.

Other information on the case firm includes the following:

➤ A central transportation department is responsible for inbound and intrafirm shipments, while the strategic business units are responsible for outbound transportation.

➤ The company employs a Materials Requirements Planning (MRP) system for planning production.

➤ Responsibilities in order management and fulfillment are divided among several departments.

➤ The firm has a supplier certification program in place.

➤ Ninety percent of components are procured off-the-shelf.

➤ Most managers in the firm come from an engineering or research and development background.

➤ Some aspects of the firm's operations, such as research and development, are centralized.

➤ The firm has experienced several years of double-digit sales and profit growth.

➤ The various product groups share common manufacturing assets.

Although the case example is a large, high-technology firm, we believe that most of the discussion is generic, applicable to the majority of companies operating in the developed world.

➤ Step 1. Collect/Analyze Baseline Data

We used the diagnostic tool in the Appendix to gather baseline data on areas of the case firm's operations in which we found symptoms of underperformance. Figure 7.1 summarizes the symptoms, problems, and root causes found in the baseline analysis.

As illustrated in Figure 7.1, the case firm is experiencing five major symptoms: high stockout levels, unprofitable customer accounts, excessive transportation costs, high levels of inventory, and high production costs. A number of problems cause each of these symptoms. For example, the high stockout levels are due to uncertainty over the size and timing of customer orders and to the inability of customers to track the status of orders at the case firm. Excessive transportation costs stem from a combination of factors. These include large numbers of rush deliveries, no coordination between inbound and outbound shipments, imbedded supplier profits in the cost of inbound transportation, the fact

Areas	Symptoms	Problems	Cross-Functional Root Causes of Supply-Chain Problems
Demand management	➤ High stockout levels. ➤ Unprofitable customer accounts.	➤ Uncertainty of the size and timing of future customer orders. ➤ No real-time tracking of order status is available to customers. ➤ Company does not offer differential levels of customer service depending on value of customers.	➤ Inaccurate demand forecasts. ➤ Actual demand information is not being fed to the MRP system. ➤ No visibility of inventory levels in the supply chain. ➤ Lack of supply-chain leadership. ➤ Logistics responsibilities are split among different departments in the company. ➤ Lack of electronic commerce capabilities across the supply chain.
Transportation management	➤ Excessive transportation costs.	➤ Rush orders and rush deliveries. ➤ No coordination between inbound and outbound shipments or between outbound shipments of different product groups.	➤ Company has been more concerned with market share than controlling supply-chain costs. ➤ Firm lacks data on shipping volumes by lane. (continues)

Figure 7.1 Analyzing baseline data: symptoms, problems and root causes.

Areas	Symptoms	Problems	Cross-Functional Root Causes of Supply-Chain Problems
		➤ Suppliers embed profits in transportation costs on goods shipped FOB destination.	➤ Company does not have systematic approach to the collection of metrics.
		➤ Customers select carriers even when firm pays transportation bill.	➤ Absence of information on customer profitability and service expectations.
		➤ Excessive number of carriers are used.	
Inventory management	➤ High levels of inventories, including high levels of slow-moving, obsolete, and otherwise excess materials and goods, and high inventory and storage costs.	➤ Inaccurate demand forecasting.	
		➤ Inefficient use of warehouse space.	
		➤ Business units do not write off and dispose of excess or obsolete inventory.	
	➤ Low inventory turnover rates.	➤ No vendor managed inventory program.	

(continues)

Figure 7.1 Continued

Areas	Symptoms	Problems	Cross-Functional Root Causes of Supply-Chain Problems
Production management	➤ High production costs.	➤ Constant rescheduling of production. ➤ Few long-term supply contracts even for those supplies deemed critical to the success of the firm.	

Figure 7.1 Continued

that customers select carriers even when the case firm pays for transportation costs, and the use of an excessive number of carriers.

A number of systematic causes underlie these problems, and the root causes span several functional and departmental areas. For example, inaccurate demand forecasts lead to uncertainty in the timing of customer orders, high uses of rush orders and deliveries, and the constant rescheduling of production—affecting the marketing, production, and purchasing departments, among others. Splitting logistics responsibilities between various units and functional areas causes a lack of coordination of inbound and outbound shipments, inefficient use of warehouse space, and the constant rescheduling of production, again affecting a number of departments.

It is clear that in order to eliminate the symptoms, the case firm must correct the problems by addressing the root causes. The benchmarking process is a powerful tool for this task.

➤ Step 2. Identify and Gather Data on Best Practices Firms

After the firm has finished gathering baseline data on its operations, the next step in the benchmarking process is to identify best practices firms. As outlined above, there are at least three levels at which benchmarking can be performed. At the lowest level, a firm can benchmark its performance metrics against best practices firms. At a higher level, a firm can benchmark its processes. At an even higher level, a firm can benchmark its strategies against best practices performers.

The choice of firms with which to benchmark depends, in part, on the level of benchmarking being undertaken. If the firm is benchmarking at the performance metric level (e.g., inventory turnover ratio), it is often best to benchmark against a leading firm in the same industry, because these metrics tend to vary considerably from industry to industry. However, at the process and strategic levels, benchmarking candidates may come from both within and outside the baseline firm's industry. For example, at the process level, the baseline firm may want to compare its electronic commerce capabilities against those of a firm in another industry, known for being a leader in the implementation of electronic commerce. Or, the company may want to benchmark its electronic commerce practices against those of the leading electronic commerce firm in its industry. At the strategic level, the baseline company may want to determine how best to increase market share by comparing its strategies to a perennial market-share leader in another industry or to the market share leader in its own industry.

The case analysis in this chapter deals with benchmarking at the process and strategic levels. This means that the baseline firm may wish to choose benchmarking candidates both within and outside its industry.

There are several ways to identify potential benchmarking candidates. In the logistics field, the annual conference of the Council of Logistics Management is often a good source of leads. This conference brings together several thousand practitioners who are often at the forefront of the logistics field. In recent years, the conference has had a benchmarking track during which firms discuss their benchmarking processes and candidates. Informal conversations during the conference can often generate leads for potential candidates. Other sources for benchmarking candidates include supply-chain consulting firms, industry trade associations, trade journals, and academic publications.

The next step is to collect data on best practices companies you identified that are comparable to your baseline information. Common methods for obtaining this information include telephone interviews, mail surveys, personal interviews, direct observations, and company publications. Other possible sources include trade publications and trade associations.

➤ Step 3. Identify and Analyze Gaps in Performance

Comparing your baseline data with benchmarking data will enable you to identify performance gaps between your firm and the performance leaders. Then, you can analyze the reasons for the gaps and begin to envision how to bridge them. Figure 7.2 presents such an analysis regarding the case example firm, drawn both from the baseline observations in Figure 7.1 and the best practices discussed in previous chapters. The case company's processes illustrate how problems and their causes have a common supply-chain platform. Because problems and their causes generate the performance symptoms, it follows that the benchmarking effort should focus on improving the processes that encompass them.

	Current Situation from Baseline Analysis	**Best Practices Procedures**
General	Logistics is a fragmented support activity with functions divided among several product divisions and the headquarters operations unit.	There is a unified, corporatewide view of logistics as a value center, allowing the best practices firms to use their logistics operations to create new business, improve operational efficiency, and lower transaction costs.
	No comprehensive plan to collect logistics cost data.	Simple and clear procedures to collect baseline data, benchmark within the firm and against other firms, and to use metrics to regularly and systematically assess performance.
Supplier management	Competition between suppliers developed by requesting current supplier—as well as two to five other potential suppliers—to supply standard components for comparison purposes.	Procurement department uses large-scale, constantly updated, fully searchable databases of standard parts and manufacturers to identify suppliers and solicit bids.
	Chooses suppliers on the basis of lowest bids. Currently has few long-term contracts even for those supplies deemed critical to the success of the firm.	Targeted approach to develop a closer relationship with fewer suppliers of items critical to the firm's operations. Creation of collaborative information systems to jointly manage inventories throughout supply channels.

Figure 7.2 Comparison of company processes to best practice procedures.

	Current Situation from Baseline Analysis	**Best Practices Procedures**
Information systems	Lack of integrated information tools. The firm does not have real-time point-of-sale data, the ability to track customer demand on a real-time basis, or EDI links with supply-chain members.	Fully integrated architecture for supply-chain management with real-time data transfers between departments within the organization and among firms in the supply chain. Aim for full implementation of paperless environment for shipment tracing, billing, and notification of receipt.
Demand management	Demand management is a fragmented function in which information from customers is not used to maximize profitability and individual product groups with no central coordination fill orders.	Demand management as an integrated process in which there is central coordination of all aspects of the customer interface including the solicitation of new business and the forecasting of sales, and customers are identified on the basis of profitability and provided with appropriate levels of service.
Transportation management	Inbound and outbound transportation activities are fragmented across the firm.	Integrated logistics operation that achieves full economies of scale and scope by combining inbound and outbound logistics into a single coordinated system. This arrangement allows the firm to save money through volume discounts.
	Many transportation decisions are made on expedited basis at premium rates with limited use of contracts.	Long-term partnerships with select carriers reduce rates as a result of better planning and scale economies.
	No documentation of freight flows and incomplete shipment cost data.	Complete database on inbound and outbound shipments with transportation costs for each movement. Flows aggregated across traffic lanes.

Figure 7.2 Continued

Figure 7.2 raises a number of specific issues. However, the major theme that seems to run through the entire logistics operations of the core firm is a lack of supply-chain focus. Logistics is currently a set of fragmented activities undertaken by various departments, mainly within the strategic business units of supply-chain member firms. As a result, transportation costs are high compared to best practices firms, as are inventory and warehousing costs, while customer service levels are below those of the best practices firms.

Further examination reveals a number of potential explanations for the fragmented approach to logistics operations. First, most managers in the firm come from an engineering or research and development background. Their emphasis is on innovating and producing better products, not on supply-chain efficiencies. Second, the firm has been formed through mergers and acquisitions, with each newly acquired department bringing its own information technology, its own product lines, its own logistics personnel, and its own corporate culture. Although management has centralized some aspects of the component companies' operations, such as research and development, they have done little to integrate the various supply chains and have been unable to unify information technology across all departments. In addition, they have created few mechanisms to facilitate and coordinate supply-chain operations among the strategic business units and between supply-chain firms. Finally, during the "good times" of past sales and profit growth, top management did not focus on the need for supply-chain improvements. However, as the markets for many of the firm's products have matured, and as profit increases have slowed, the importance of controlling supply-chain costs has become clear.

Although the gap analysis did not explicitly assess the human resources of the case firm, it is reasonable to assume that severe managerial and operational deficits exist in the supply-chain function. New hires, training programs, or contracting for supply-chain services can overcome these deficits. However, not only is the firm currently lacking a cadre of well-trained supply-chain personnel, but the few who are in place are probably consumed with day-to-day operational problems. The firm also lacks a chief logistics or supply-chain officer to provide leadership in this area. As a result, no one is providing strategic direction on supply-chain matters.

The firm's incentive system has no mechanism for rewarding employees based on total supply-chain performance. Until the incentives are changed to reflect the new priorities, the production department may still be incentivized to arrange schedules to minimize production costs— without regard for the impact of these schedules on procurement and distribution. Other departments may, likewise, continue to optimize operations within their own departments without regard to the rest of the company or to other firms in the supply chain.

Finally, the gap analysis reveals glaring weaknesses in the case company's information technology. The lack of visibility in inventory management throughout the supply chain, for example, results in poor demand forecasting, which in turn has negative impacts on production scheduling and procurement. Integrating information technology across the firm and the supply chain will undoubtedly prove difficult—a major reason that many firms use third-party providers for this task.

➤ Step 4. Develop a Plan to Reengineer Your Processes

Now that the performance gaps are clear, the case company must develop a plan to reengineer its process to close the gaps and improve performance. In this section, we provide suggestions for a plan to close the gaps identified in Figure 7.2.

1. General Gaps

The case firm has two important general performance gaps. First, the organizational structure of the firms is fragmented. Second, the firm lacks a comprehensive plan to collect logistics cost data. To realize the competitive advantages best practices companies enjoy, the case firm needs to develop an integrated supply-chain strategy. A key component of this strategy is having a logistics leader. One possibility is that an existing executive, such as a vice president of operations, could become the supply-chain leader for the firm. The vice president of operations is often well-positioned to exercise the proper cross-functional leadership. Better coordination will result in lower direct transportation charges (through greater realization of quantity discounts, fewer empty backhauls, more truckload shipments, etc.); improved customer service (through, for example, improved coordination of commitment to delivery with manufacturing); and lower inventories (through better management/tracking of material flows through the system).

We also recommend that the firm establish a management-level supply-chain steering team, with cross-functional participation. The vice president of operations could direct this effort. The steering team would review supply-chain processes and provide recommendations for changes, with special emphasis on the impact of one department's processes on the operations of other departments. As a second step, the team could consider involving participants from other supply-chain members. Among other tasks, a supply-chain steering team could direct the collection of metrics and monitor these metrics to check on the evolution of low-performance symptoms.

2. Supplier Management Gaps

The gap analysis revealed a number of major problems with supplier management. The firm appears to use a large variety of suppliers, but does not have a modern, technology-based process to solicit competitive bids among suppliers. As well, the firm has not differentiated between those firms that supply commodity parts and those firms that supply nonstandard and critical components. With the first group of suppliers, it is often best to develop processes that minimize price. However, with the second group of suppliers, long-term contracts that guarantee supply may be more appropriate. With these thoughts in mind, the following recommendations to close performance gaps may be in order:

➤ *Investigate the adoption of new information tools that facilitate the search for suppliers.* It is possible, in a number of industries, to use large-scale, constantly updated, fully searchable databases to search for standard supplies. Using these databases should both reduce the search time involved in locating supply sources and increase the pool of potential suppliers. For example, a number of supplier databases contain detailed and searchable supplier information, such as Dunn & Bradstreet ratings, production data, and so on. These databases can automatically generate e-mail requests for quotes directed to selected suppliers. Some can also allow buyers to prepare bid packages, select suppliers, and post packages to a secure Web site; allow suppliers to receive initial bid packages and to prepare and post bids; and allow for multiround bids to be conducted on line. Most major enterprise resource planning (ERP) providers plan to integrate Internet-based procurement into their products by the year 2000.

➤ *Institute a cross-functional, team-based approach to manage the prequalification of potential suppliers.* Use this team to solicit all requests for quotes (RFQs), and evaluate all supplier bids using a common procedure across the firm. The goal should be to create and maintain a more efficient vendor base with several alternative suppliers for major commodity supplies, and to inject greater competition into the bidding process for commodity products while ensuring availability of supply as needed.

➤ *Focus on building strategic sourcing partnerships with critical suppliers as part of a clearer segmentation of the supplier base.* For those buys that are more "strategic" and of higher value, the firm needs a more targeted approach that aims to cultivate and monitor fewer partners. The overall goal should be to reduce the number of suppliers of critical parts while concurrently increasing the firm's importance to key suppliers. This approach can make the suppliers more responsive and flexible in meeting firm needs. A focus on supplier partnerships has been a best business practice for many years.

➤ *Develop better information links with key suppliers.* Information links facilitate the development of collaborative information systems that allow supply-chain partners to review on-hand inventories across the supply chain and move to a more continual replenishment pattern, slash the order-to-receipt cycle time on purchased components, provide in-transit visibility for ordered parts, and automate payment transactions. An intranet open to core suppliers may also be appropriate. For example, Ford has opened its intranet to major suppliers. This enables suppliers to see in detail not only the specific stock Ford has on hand and the number of units that will be needed, but also in what sequence of colors the next shipment of car seats should be packed.

➤ *Establish a vendor-managed inventory (VMI) program,* allowing suppliers to assume greater responsibilities for inventory management and replenishment of the firm's inventories. A good early target for VMI is often the maintenance repair and operations supply base, which can account for up to 30 percent of a firm's supply costs and is generally quite amenable to continual replenishment concepts.

3. *Logistics Information Systems Gaps*

The gap analysis in Figure 7.2 revealed that the firm lacks the decision-support systems and executive information tools needed to give decision-makers timely supply-chain information. As a result, supply-chain costs are higher than they should be, and performance is substandard. The firm needs to integrate the flow of information throughout the supply chain by using common software programs whenever possible. The firm can also investigate the use of integrated supply-chain operational software programs and/or enterprise resource planning tools that will enable effective management of information flows within the organization.

It is also important to synchronize information flow actions. For example, the receipt of customer orders must be synchronized with the planning of inventory levels and the planning of shipments. Through the coordination of information flows, the firm will be able to handle higher volumes of information at lower costs.

4. *Demand Management Gaps*

Figure 7.2 revealed that the firm's demand management is a fragmented function in which customer orders are filled by individual product groups with no central coordination. The company also does a poor job of differentiating between its highly profitable customers and its unprofitable customers. A good demand management program can reduce supply-chain costs and ensure that high-yield customers get priority service to encourage repeat business. In some cases, service to low-yield customers may have to be sacrificed to meet the needs of those 20 percent of customers that are likely to be generating 80 percent of the firm's profits. The airline industry, with a large array of price and service offerings, is a good example of demand management in action.

In this context, we make the following recommendations for improvement:

➤ *Conduct a thorough examination of the firm's current customer list to determine the profitability of each customer.* Increase the service levels available to the most profitable customers by offering greater choices in distribution options, including more timely delivery schedules. Work with the production department so that orders for the most profitable customers are met before other, less profitable orders. Examine ways of reducing the costs of providing products to the least profitable customers, for example, through greater consolidation in distribution. Delay both production and distribution to the least profitable customers in order to smooth out production and delivery schedules.

➤ *When seeking new customers, do a more thorough job in determining their potential profitability,* perhaps through the use of outside vendors to compile prospect lists to contact and rate prospects, and to pass on high-value referrals to the sales force. A number of high-technology firms are taking this approach, relying on third-party providers for their prospect databases and on local telemarketing firms for the actual prospecting. Traditional sales forces often resist new and more scientific marketing methods, so it will be important for senior management to champion the new approaches aggressively.

➤ *Build "real-time windows" into the inventory levels of key distributors* by gaining access to their intranets. Flow through demand information to the firm's suppliers as expeditiously as possible.

➤ *Establish more collaborative forecasting relationships with distributors* to increase the accuracy of demand forecasts. One collaborative possibility would be to use emerging Internet-based applications to alert supply-chain partners to unexpected variations in supply-chain processes, such as out-of-stock items, excess inventory, and changes in delivery schedules.

5. Transportation Management Gaps

Figure 7.2 revealed a number of performance gaps in the case firm's transportation management. Inbound and outbound transportation activities are fragmented across the firm, which has only a limited number of contracts with transportation carriers. Other concerns include excessive use of premium transportation, a lack of documentation of freight flows, and incomplete shipment cost data. Given these problems, and others, we make the following recommendations:

➤ *Gather information on shipments to negotiate more effectively with carriers for volume reductions.* Specifically, develop a comprehensive database to identify potential savings on various shipping lanes. This would include identifying shipment consolidation potential among various customers.

➤ *Combine volume lane information to identify additional savings opportunities* when inbound, outbound, inter-plant, and warehouse-to-warehouse traffic move over similar lanes. Negotiate volume discounts with carriers on a request-for-quotation (RFQ) basis over inbound and outbound lanes.

➤ *Form a team of representatives from the head office and from the various business groups* to develop an integrated transportation strategy to: (1) combine shipments among the groups when feasible, and (2) share transportation assets to reduce logistics costs.

➤ *Charge low-yield customers for premium transportation services* when they request those services. Minimize customer selection of carriers when the firm is paying the freight charges.

➤ *Whenever profitable, change the terms of trade for inbound shipping to FOB origin.* A program combining FOB origin shipments with a smaller, more selective carrier base should lower inbound transportation costs.

➤ *If not already doing so, use a third-party firm that specializes in auditing freight bills.* For most firms, third-party freight auditors can monitor freight payments more effectively than can be done in-house.

Step 5. Implement the Reengineering Plan

It is now important to develop a plan for putting best practices/performance improvement recommendations into action, and then execute that plan. This process usually involves reengineering some or all of the processes involved. As noted earlier, a number of considerations are important to developing a reengineering plan, including:

➤ *Prioritizing the reengineering effort.* Firms can prioritize their recommendations based on a precise quantification of resource requirements, cost, time, and customer value. They can use standard financial techniques, such as net present value or cost-benefit analysis, to determine which recommendations provide the greatest payback. However, it is evident that some of our recommendations ought to be carried out before others. For example, before new software is purchased to correct some of the current information technology deficits, a team should be put into place, as outlined above, to choose the most appropriate software. Project planning software tools are helpful in developing timelines for implementation and coordinating efforts among the various processes to be reengineered.

➤ *Obtaining management buy-in for the plan.* Projects with the most visibility to top management—generally those that provide quick cost savings or revenue improvements—often receive the highest priority in a reengineering plan. Among our recommendations for the case firm, steps to improve transportation management by consolidating shipments among fewer carriers are often associated with quick cost savings. Carriers are generally willing to provide large discounts to shippers that can provide volumes, and the case firm is currently not receiving these discounts.

➤ *Making insourcing versus outsourcing decisions.* One of the most important decisions is whether a firm should insource or outsource a process. This decision should not be made until baseline data are collected and the gap analysis performed. Otherwise, the firm will not be able to assess the performance of the third-party firm, should the decision be made to outsource.

The most important criteria for making an insourcing/outsourcing decision are whether the process to be outsourced is core to the firm; the internal capabilities of the firm in regard to the outsourcing company; and, perhaps most importantly, the cost savings and customer improvements that the third-party can offer. Non-core activities for which the firm has few managerial capabilities and that require an investment in costly technology are good candidates for outsourcing (e.g., vehicle maintenance and repair). On the other hand, all core activities should remain insourced unless there are extremely compelling arguments to the contrary.

➤ *Considering potential synergies or diseconomies between the processes.* Reengineering certain processes together produces greater gains than reengineering them individually. As explained above, eliminating performance gaps in different functional areas depends upon eliminating the causes generating those performance gaps. Indeed, the implementation of benchmarking plans to optimize the use of human, physical, and financial resources in the supply chain will be most cost-effective when it combines supply-chain functional areas with active flows of goods and information. For example, demand forecasts are used to plan production and purchases, which are, in turn, linked to inventory levels and transportation planning. By addressing inaccurate demand forecasts, a firm can reengineer processes in these interconnected functional areas to correct multiple low-performance symptoms (e.g., excessive stockouts, high transportation costs due to rush deliveries, and high production costs due to frequent changeovers in manufacturing lines).

➤ *Aligning the benchmarking plan with overall firm strategy.* Hayes and Pisana[3] argue that benchmarking programs leading to performance-level improvements should build new capabilities for the overall competitiveness of the firm. For example, consider a plant that establishes a goal of drastically reducing its inventories and lead times. It can approach this goal either by adopting an MRP-type system or by adopting a JIT pull system. As Hayes and Pisana state:

Adopting an MRP system fosters skills in using computers and managing databases ... Pull systems ... encourage skills in factory floor problem solving, incremental process improvement, and fast response. Each approach ... leaves the organization with a different set of skills and thus a different set of strategic options in the future. A decision about which approach to pursue should not be made without considering which set of capabilities would be most valuable to the company.[3]

Most supply-chain processes cut across departments within a firm and several require the involvement of more than one firm in a supply chain. The case study, for example, identified transportation management as a problem. The company is not coordinating its inbound and outbound shipments, nor is it consolidating shipments among the various departments in the organization. An integrated transportation strategy requires the involvement of suppliers and distributors, as well as purchasing, distribution, marketing personnel from headquarters and the various business groups within the firm.

Obviously, reengineering the firm's transportation processes will be a team effort. Most books on reengineering point to the importance of having a team leader in the reengineering process. The leader must be senior enough to direct the reengineering efforts and counter the resistance that often arises from departments that feel they will lose resources or staff as a result of the process. Often a chief logistics officer or manager at the vice president level is in the best position to lead the reengineering effort.

In general, some principles to follow in a reengineering effort include the following:

➤ Secure participation from all departments that will be affected by the reengineering effort.

➤ Ensure that suppliers, distributors, carriers, and other supply-chain members participate when their efforts are needed to make the reengineering effort a success.

➤ Appoint a senior manager with cross-functional or cross-departmental authority as a team leader.

➤ Involve as many personnel at both the managerial level and the operational level as possible to ensure buy-in.

➤ Use as transparent an effort as possible. Do not try to disguise or hide changes from personnel to be affected.

■ BENCHMARKING TO IMPROVE YOUR COMPANY'S PERFORMANCE

Chapters 6 and 7 and the supply-chain diagnostic tool in the Appendix provide a complete set of tools and procedures for baselining and benchmarking your firm's operations. Of course, each firm is unique, and you will need to adapt the tools and procedures to your own situation. Using the approaches outlined is more than a planning exercise, and they take time, resources, and commitment to complete. However, we have found in our own research and consulting practices that these tools and procedures can work to improve organizational performance. Many of the companies you choose as benchmark leaders used these approaches to get where you want to be.

Chapter

Moving Toward the Truly Extended Enterprise

Business today is at a crossroads. Companies around the world have done a great deal to take cost out of their operations, to downsize and reengineer in the hopes of becoming more agile and competitive. They have discovered, however, that these kinds of internally directed changes will take them only so far. To jump to the next level of success, they must look beyond their corporate boundaries—to their supply chains. They must learn how to manage these chains—or extended enterprises—as single, albeit huge, living organisms. They must break through traditional inter-and intraorganizational barriers, which serve only to hamstring enterprises as they move toward globalization.

Never before has there been so much pressure for companies to achieve synergies, both internally and externally. These synergies are possible, and indeed vital in four major areas:

1. *Between core internal functions,* including everything from forecasting and production planning, procurement,

manufacturing, transportation and distribution management, inventory management, and customer service, to sales
and marketing, finance, and strategic planning. The aim of
successfully orchestrating all of these areas is to accelerate
and coordinate decision making, speed up the operational
response to the pull of demand, satisfy customers more fully
and, ultimately, gain market dominance. Companies can no
longer afford to manage in a context of isolated, vertical functional silos. Such an approach is a costly anachronism.

Our research findings on supply-chain best practices
clearly validate this point. As Chapter 2 reports, best practices firms typically integrate the disparate supply-chain
functions (which are spread among a number of departments), either formally or informally. As a result of this
horizontal integration, these enterprises achieve significant
synergies within the organization. These synergies, in turn,
generate sizable savings in inventory and logistics/trans-
portation costs, reduce resource consumption (both human
and infrastructure), boost productivity, speed product to
market, shorten the design cycle, and much more. Studies
show that best-in-class leaders in supply-chain management
can have as much as a 50 percent advantage over median
competitors. That's a remarkable competitive edge.

2. *Between internal and external supply-chain actors.*
Leading companies orchestrate not only their own activities
and capabilities, but also those of their supply-chain partners (i.e., suppliers/vendors, service providers, alliance
partners, and customers). This orchestration requires the
enterprise to have very sophisticated knowledge and understanding of its supply-chain partners. This understanding
encompasses organizational structures and capabilities,
physical network assets, technology/information management systems, and so on.

3. *Between the enterprise and its supply-chain partners—
core customers and suppliers.* Best practices companies are
establishing collaborative forecasting and planning efforts

that span the supply chain. These firms realize that they can no longer afford to plan in a vacuum and constantly surprise internal departments, external suppliers, service providers, and even customers with unplanned or unannounced decisions or events. Collaborative planning is a potential goldmine for companies, allowing them to eliminate expensive buffer inventories, improve customer order fulfillment, optimize assets and, in general, boost performance and profits.

4. *Between physical and electronic channels.* Effective linkages between the physical and information pipelines are imperative in order to realize the greatest benefits from supply-chain integration. Only by having real-time or near-real-time visibility across the supply chain can an enterprise optimize both its processes and resources—and those of its supply-chain partners. Pipeline visibility reduces and in many cases eliminates the need for physical assets. It also helps firms better deploy those assets that are needed.

Overall, the enterprise must pursue synergies in every aspect of its business in order to succeed in its ruthless and constant search for leverage in the marketplace. Today, leading companies have only begun to tap the potential of integrated supply-chain management. They have extended their enterprises to enfold only one or two outside trading partners or suppliers.

As we enter the twenty-first century, however, competitive pressures will necessitate a much broader span of interrelationships, implemented at a much faster pace. In fact, several specific trends will fuel these changes.

■ DRIVERS OF CHANGE

Several major forces currently at work will drive the trend toward extended enterprise management, and in so doing, heighten the demand for world-class supply-chain management capabilities. First, the *trend toward globalization* is accelerating and will continue to do so as new or underdeveloped markets come on line. More and more companies will have no choice but to view themselves in a global context—one that offers many more sourcing options and distribution points. This global context also redefines competition to include any enterprise, anywhere in the world, that can marshal the resources to serve a particular market.

The trend toward globalization, by its very nature, adds new layers of complexity to corporate supply chains. This complexity takes many shapes and forms: SKU proliferation, longer procurement and delivery pipelines, a greater number of business partners, cultural and business practice differences, information systems complexity, and many more. Managing supply-chain complexity effectively will be one of the biggest challenges faced by companies and their management teams.

To meet this challenge, companies must have access to expanded supply-chain decision support/optimization models. These models must broaden in scope to accommodate the greater diversity of sourcing and distribution parameters discussed above. Additionally, these optimization tools will need to evolve away from the static models of today, toward more real-time systems.

A number of economic pressures related to globalization will also have significant impacts on the emergence and well-being of extended enterprises. These factors include the following:

➤ Economic downturns, upheavals and currency devaluations in Asia and Russia, and continued underdevelopment in Africa and Latin America imply that sourcing low-cost labor and material, and/or locating or contracting production sites in those places, will remain important cost-cutting options for Organization for Economic Cooperation and Development (industrialized nations) corporations.

➤ The ramping-up of the new European Union will lead to a greatly enlarged and unified marketplace, demanding greater visibility and significance of supply-chain networks as cross-border activities expand.

➤ The emergence of new megamarkets (e.g., China and India) will offer unprecedented sales and growth opportunities to firms capable of jumping quickly and effectively into these markets. Expansion into these areas naturally adds complexity to already far-flung supply chains.

In response to the pressures of globalization, we are witnessing the birth of the truly global third-party logistics company. Overtaxed by the complexity of global operations, more and more companies are seeking outside help in the form of third-party logistics service providers. They realize that the new global marketplace requires sophisticated management information systems and logistics infrastructures that deliver speed, flexibility, accuracy, and precision in supply-chain processes. As reported in Chapters 3 and 4, it is no surprise that the trend toward logistics/supply-chain outsourcing has been gaining momentum steadily over the past decade. Companies are facing the fact that the requirements of today's logistics systems exceed the capabilities of their logistics staff and infrastructure. And the ever-quickening pace of technological change makes it difficult for many companies to keep up with, much less get out in front of, their information system requirements.

Not only are more companies outsourcing their logistics activities, but more companies are outsourcing more of their supply chain. In fact, there appears to be a growing trend toward outsourcing virtually all supply-chain functions. Our research into best practices in logistics outsourcing found that those companies that outsource their total supply chain realize significant savings—over 20 percent the first year, and 15 percent in subsequent years.

We are witnessing the rise of an elite corps of third-party logistics companies equipped with the necessary managerial breadth and depth, the financial and technological resources, and the requisite networks of regional logistics partnerships to provide integrated cross-functional supply-chain outsourcing. In order to serve customers globally, these third parties are forming close strategic alliances with logistics service firms around the world. While working relationships of one kind or another are not new to the logistics/transportation world, technology advances allow today's alliances to be closer and better synchronized than was ever before possible. Hence, companies feel more confident outsourcing some or all of their supply chains than ever before.

Finally, in terms of major forces fueling the evolution toward the extended enterprise, one cannot overlook the *Intelligent Connectivity Infrastructure*. This infrastructure takes several forms: the Internet, intranets, extranets, electronic data interchange (EDI), emerging extensible mark up language (XML) standards, and new publish and subscribe messaging technology. Over the next two decades, this Intelligent Connectivity Infrastructure will proliferate as access-enabling technology becomes cheaper and more widely available. Technology systems that integrate highly interactive multimedia Web site front ends with secure EDI back office functions will serve as important transitional technology systems until truly net-centric, open electronic commerce standards prevail.

■ TOWARD THE TWENTY-FIRST-CENTURY ENTERPRISE

These forces of change all point to the need for specific actions to facilitate the transformation to a twenty-first-century extended enterprise. These actions include:

➤ Appointment of a high-level, empowered executive authority (be it an individual or a team) to manage logistics/supply-chain activities across organizational levels and functional areas.

➤ Development and execution of a full-scale extended-enterprise vision, and the strategy and tactics needed to realize that vision.

➤ Rapidly piloting and ramping up extended enterprise initiatives.

➤ New-style centralization of supply-chain management across the multiple functions and levels of the firm.

➤ Urgent and continuous organizational innovations in supply-chain design and management.

➤ Constant evaluation of internal supply-chain capabilities and the associated cost/benefits of retaining those capabilities in-house versus outsourcing them.

To begin the process of reengineering toward an extended enterprise model, management must assess its own organizational performance, as well as that of its partners. Management must baseline and benchmark the extended enterprise's current performance levels, set new objectives, implement improvement actions, monitor performance for compliance with target objectives and, finally, take corrective steps in a timely manner.

Chapters 6 and 7 provide an initial roadmap and tool with which to execute this analysis. The two chapters offer processes the reader can use to benchmark against best practices strategies and structure paths for improvement.

In summary, we have attempted to give readers information that is truly useful as companies move toward the extended-enterprise model. We describe what constitutes a world-class logistics/supply-chain organization structure, how to conduct a supply-chain self-assessment, how to organize to implement logistics best practices, how to evaluate outsourcing, and how and where to extend the boundaries of an organization. In essence, the book constitutes a systems integration activity that draws on the best of the available external and internal inputs to create a finely tuned competitive business entity—one that will thrive in the twenty-first century.

Appendix

Supply-Chain Diagnostic Tool

The following interview instrument will contribute to the collecting of important information about your firm's supply-chain activities. The instrument is divided into four major sections. The first section seeks general information about your company's most critical logistics problems and improvement objectives. The second section seeks information about the overall configuration of your firm's supply chain. The third section includes questions that will help you measure the efficiency of the logistics operations and supply-chain partners associated with each of your key products. The fourth section seeks information about your firm's logistics management practices. Finally, the fifth section seeks information about your perception of your company's logistics efficiency in multiple levels of your firm's supply chain.

■ SUPPLY CHAIN DIAGNOSTIC

➤ I. Client Orientation

1. What are the critical *symptoms* of supply-chain problems you are presently experiencing?

_____

_____

_____

_____

2. What do you believe are the *underlying problems* causing these symptoms?

_____
_____
_____
_____

3. Can you identify any *root causes* of these problems?

_____
_____
_____
_____

4. What has been done or proposed to be done to address these problems up until now?

_____
_____
_____
_____

5. What are your key objectives in this assignment?

_____
_____
_____
_____

6. What are the key economic, technological, social, and regulatory forces driving the logistics/supply-chain management environment in your industry?

_____
_____
_____
_____

7. How do you see these forces affecting your own practices in logistics/supply-chain management now and in the future?

_____
_____
_____
_____

➤ II. Supply-Chain Products/Information Flows

1. Please define your overall portfolio of products and services:

_____

_____

_____

_____

2. List core products and percentage of total revenue accounted for by each:

Core Product	Percentage of Total Revenue

3. Respondents should fill out an operations assessment *for each core product* previously identified.

_____

_____

_____

_____

➤ III. Operations Assessment (by Each Core Product)

CORE PRODUCT: _____

A. *Profile of Customers*
1. Who are your key customers?

_____

_____

_____

2. What percentage of demand do these key customers account for?

_____
_____
_____
_____

3. How would you define the customer order cycle and the nature of demand for this product? (Describe seasonality issues and other causes of spikes in demand):

_____
_____
_____
_____

4. How do you manage demand for this product?

_____
_____
_____
_____

A. Do you use continual replenishment based on real-time point-of-sales data? (If yes, please describe):

_____
_____
_____
_____

B. Do you use quarterly or other types of forecasting? (If yes, please describe):

_____
_____
_____
_____

5. How do you get access to information about customer purchasing patterns for your forecasts?

_____
_____
_____
_____

6. What other sources of market information do you use to better pinpoint future demand for this product?

_____

_____

_____

_____

7. How would you rate your accuracy in predicting demand spikes or other unusual market events?

_____

_____

_____

_____

8. Do you use any kind of asset-tracking technology for inventory management and in-transit visibility? (If yes, please describe):

_____

_____

_____

_____

9. What software tools and electronic commerce tools (including the Internet) are in use to interact with customers or to mine market data?

_____

_____

_____

_____

10. How do you track and measure customer service? What metrics do you use?

_____

_____

_____

_____

B. Profile of Competitors

11. Who do you consider are your most important competitors in this industry?

_____

_____

_____
_____
_____

12. Are your competitors' logistics strategies and managerial practices different from your firm's? (If yes, please explain):

_____
_____
_____
_____

13. Do you perceive the need to examine critical logistics practices of your competitors? (If yes, please explain):

_____
_____
_____
_____

C. Profile of Distribution System

14. Types of channels to customers:

_____
_____
_____
_____

A. Where are your key retail outlets?

_____
_____
_____
_____

B. Where are your key wholesalers/distributors located?

_____
_____
_____
_____

15. What are your key shipping lanes linking your distribution facilities with retail and wholesale outlets?

_____
_____
_____
_____

16. For each lane described in question 15, please indicate the annual volume of product shipped, the transportation modes used, and customer satisfaction with delivery times.

Shipping Lanes (O/D)	Annual Shipping Volumes	Modes Used	Percent of Annual Shipping Volumes	Customer Satisfaction with Delivery Times
		Air Freight		
		Truckload Freight		
		Less-than-Truckload Freight		
		Intermodal		
		Air Freight		
		Truckload Freight		
		Less-than-Truckload Freight		
		Intermodal		
		Air Freight		
		Truckload Freight		
		Less-than-Truckload Freight		
		Intermodal		
		Air Freight		
		Truckload Freight		
		Less-than-Truckload Freight		
		Intermodal		
		Air Freight		
		Truckload Freight		

Shipping Lanes (O/D)	Annual Shipping Volumes	Modes Used	Percent of Annual Shipping Volumes	Customer Satisfaction with Delivery Times
		Less-than-Truckload Freight		
		Intermodal		
		Air Freight		
		Truckload Freight		
		Less-than-Truckload Freight		
		Intermodal		

D. Profile of Production

17. What are the locations of your key production points?

_____
_____
_____
_____

18. Briefly describe the production process:
A. What are the products or services provided by each of your firm's plants?

_____
_____
_____
_____

B. Do you produce to order? Do you produce to inventory?

_____
_____
_____
_____

C. Do you have to accommodate many production process changes per week in the dedicated production facility for this product?

_____

_____

_____

_____

D. What are your product lead times?

_____

_____

_____

_____

E. How many inventory turns per year do you average?

_____

_____

_____

_____

F. How much inventory is in work in progress, finished goods, and raw materials?

_____

_____

_____

_____

G. How much are your average work-in-process carrying costs?

_____

_____

_____

_____

H. For each unit of this product, what are the key cost drivers?

_____

_____

_____

_____

I. How long is an average generation of this product?

_____

_____

_____

_____

19. For each lane linking your production facilities with your distribution centers, please indicate the annual volume of product transported, the transportation modes used, and your level of satisfaction with the current transportation times.

Shipping Lanes (O/D)	Annual Volumes	Modes Used	Percent of Annual Volumes	Satisfaction with Transportation Times
		Air Freight		
		Truckload Freight		
		Less-than-Truckload Freight		
		Intermodal		
		Air Freight		
		Truckload Freight		
		Less-than-Truckload Freight		
		Intermodal		
		Air Freight		
		Truckload Freight		
		Less-than-Truckload Freight		
		Intermodal		
		Air Freight		
		Truckload Freight		
		Less-than-Truckload Freight		

Shipping Lanes (O/D)	Annual Volumes	Modes Used	Percent of Annual Volumes	Satisfaction with Transportation Times
		Intermodal		
		Air Freight		
		Truckload Freight		
		Less-than-Truckload Freight		
		Intermodal		
		Air Freight		
		Truckload Freight		
		Less-than-Truckload Freight		
		Intermodal		

E. Profile of Suppliers

20. Who are your suppliers?

_____
_____
_____
_____

21. Where are they located?

_____
_____
_____
_____

22. How are they selected?

_____
_____
_____
_____

23. How much lead time do you give suppliers in your ordering process?

_____

_____

_____

_____

24. For each lane linking your production facilities with your suppliers, please indicate the annual volume of materials transported, the transportation modes used, and your level of satisfaction with the current transportation times.

Shipping Lanes (O/D)	Annual Volumes	Modes Used	Percent of Annual Volumes	Satisfaction with Transportation Times
		Air Freight		
		Truckload Freight		
		Less-than-Truckload Freight		
		Intermodal		
		Air Freight		
		Truckload Freight		
		Less-than-Truckload Freight		
		Intermodal		
		Air Freight		
		Truckload Freight		
		Less-than-Truckload Freight		
		Intermodal		
		Air Freight		
		Truckload Freight		
		Less-than-Truckload Freight		

Shipping Lanes (O/D)	Annual Volumes	Modes Used	Percent of Annual Volumes	Satisfaction with Transportation Times
		Intermodal		
		Air Freight		
		Truckload Freight		
		Less-than-Truckload Freight		
		Intermodal		
		Air Freight		
		Truckload Freight		
		Less-than-Truckload Freight		
		Intermodal		

IV. Supply Chain Management Practices

A. *Organization of the Supply Management Function*

1. Based on your company's characteristics, please indicate what level in your organization is in charge of *planning and organizing* each of the outbound logistics functions listed below. (Circle one number for each item.)

Outbound Logistics Function	Level in your organization in charge of planning and organizing each of the following outbound logistics functions			
	Point-of-Sales Level	Manu-facturing Site Level	SBU Level	Head-quarters Level
Outbound Transportation	1	2	3	4
Carrier Selection	1	2	3	4
Mode Selection	1	2	3	4
Freight Payments	1	2	3	4

Outbound Logistics Function	Level in your organization in charge of planning and organizing each of the following outbound logistics functions			
	Point-of-Sales Level	Manu-facturing Site Level	SBU Level	Head-quarters Level
Warehouse Configurations and Locations	1	2	3	4
Distribution Center Con-figurations and Locations	1	2	3	4
Work-in-Process Inventory	1	2	3	4
Finished-Goods Inventory	1	2	3	4
Parts/Service Support	1	2	3	4
Product Returns	1	2	3	4
Product Handling	1	2	3	4
Packaging	1	2	3	4
Order Processing	1	2	3	4
Demand Forecasting	1	2	3	4

2. Based on your company's characteristics, please indicate what level in your organization is in charge of *operating* each of the outbound logistics functions listed below. (Circle one for each item.)

Outbound Logistics Function	Level in your organization in charge of operating each of the following outbound logistics functions			
	Point-of-Sales Level	Manu-facturing Site Level	SBU Level	Head-quarters Level
Outbound Transportation	1	2	3	4
Carrier Selection	1	2	3	4
Mode Selection	1	2	3	4
Freight Payments	1	2	3	4
Warehouse Configurations and Locations	1	2	3	4
Distribution Center Con-figurations and Locations	1	2	3	4
Work-in-Process Inventory	1	2	3	4

(continues)

Outbound Logistics Function	Level in your organization in charge of operating each of the following outbound logistics functions			
	Point-of-Sales Level	Manu-facturing Site Level	SBU Level	Head-quarters Level
Finished-Goods Inventory	1	2	3	4
Parts/Service Support	1	2	3	4
Product Returns	1	2	3	4
Product Handling	1	2	3	4
Packaging	1	2	3	4
Order Processing	1	2	3	4
Demand Forecasting	1	2	3	4

3. Based on your company's characteristics, please indicate what level in your organization is in charge of *monitoring and controlling* each of the outbound logistics functions listed below. (Circle one for each item.)

Outbound Logistics Function	Level in your organization in charge of monitoring and controlling each of the following outbound logistics functions			
	Point-of-Sales Level	Manu-facturing Site Level	SBU Level	Head-quarters Level
Outbound Transportation	1	2	3	4
Carrier Selection	1	2	3	4
Mode Selection	1	2	3	4
Freight Payments	1	2	3	4
Warehouse Configurations and Locations	1	2	3	4
Distribution Center Con-figurations and Locations	1	2	3	4
Work-in-Process Inventory	1	2	3	4
Finished-Goods Inventory	1	2	3	4
Parts/Service Support	1	2	3	4
Product Returns	1	2	3	4
Product Handling	1	2	3	4
Packaging	1	2	3	4

(continues)

Outbound Logistics Function	Level in your organization in charge of monitoring and controlling each of the following outbound logistics functions			
	Point-of-Sales Level	Manu-facturing Site Level	SBU Level	Head-quarters Level
Order Processing	1	2	3	4
Demand Forecasting	1	2	3	4

B. Structure and Division of Responsibilities

4. How is the supply-chain function managed in your organization?

_____
_____
_____
_____

5. How are responsibilities in managing the supply chain divided between headquarters and strategic business units?

_____
_____
_____
_____

C. Carrier Management

6. Are your inbound and outbound shipment volumes aggregated to attain volume discounts in negotiations with carriers?

_____
_____
_____
_____

7. Do you take title of shipments you order at the supplier's factory gate and choose carriers?

_____
_____
_____
_____

8. Do you segregate out all your freight costs and can you identify all your freight costs?

_____

_____

_____

_____

9. How often do you audit freight bills?

_____

_____

_____

_____

10. Do you use EDI for shipment invoicing and payments?

_____

_____

_____

_____

11. Do you have a system for attaining in-transit visibility of goods?

_____

_____

_____

_____

12. How do you monitor carrier performance? What metrics do you use?

_____

_____

_____

_____

13. Do you have any multiyear partnerships with carriers in place? (If yes, how do you control these partnerships? How do you measure the effectiveness of these partnerships? What metrics do you use?):

_____

_____

_____

_____

14. Do you currently outsource or have you investigated outsourcing carrier management and transportation to a third-party logistics company?

_____
_____
_____
_____

D. Supplier Management

15. How do you select suppliers?

_____
_____
_____
_____

16. Are you part of corporatewide purchasing agreements that use specific suppliers?

_____
_____
_____
_____

17. Do you use quality partnerships with core suppliers?

_____
_____
_____
_____

18. How do you measure the effectiveness of these partnerships? What metrics do you use?

_____
_____
_____
_____

19. Do you use electronic tools for supplier management? (Check the ones that apply):

_____ Post online RFQs to and receive online bids from a pool of prequalified suppliers.

_____ Use electronic catalogues to display your suppliers' products in a standard format for internal employee purchasing.

_____ Use EDI to send purchase orders, receive advance-shipping notices, and pay invoices.

_____ Use third-party supplier management firms to screen the universe of suppliers and assure best pricing?

_____ Other (please describe):

_____

_____

_____

_____

Notes

■ **CHAPTER 1**

[1]T. Nishiguchi, "Strategic Industrial Sourcing: The Japanese Advantage," Oxford University Press, 1994, pp. 204–207.

[2]The Performance Measurement Group, a subsidiary of Pittiglio Rabin Todd & McGrath, "Integrated Supply-Chain Benchmarking Study," 1997, pp. 1–8

[3]James Masters and Terrance Pohlen, Chapter 2: The Evolution of the Logistics Profession, "The Logistics Handbook," by James Robeson & William Copacino, The Free Press, New York, pp. 13–31.

[4]Ira Magaziner, White House Report on E-Commerce, excerpt from "Bringing Asia On Line", *The New York Times,* April 13, 1998, p. D1.

[5]Mosaic Group, "The Global Diffusion Of Internet Project," March 1998, p. 3.

[6]Erasmus Murphy, "A Model for Establishment of an Internet Infrastructure Within the African Continent," Internet Society, June 1997, pp. 1–20.

[7]Lisa H. Harrington, "Software for a Tough Task," *Industry Week,* September 15, 1997, pp. 20–24.

[8]Ibid.

[9]Lisa H. Harrington, "Taking Integration to the Next Level," *Transportation & Distribution,* August 1995, pp. 26–28.

■ CHAPTER 2

[1]Michael E. Porter, "Competitive Advantage: Creating and Sustaining Superior Performance," New York Free Press, 1985.

[2]John J. Coyle, Edward J. Bardi, and C. John Langley Jr., "The Management of Business Logistics," Sixth Edition, Minneapolis, West Publishing Company, 1996.

■ CHAPTER 3

[1]John L. Kent and Daniel J. Flint, "Perspectives on the Evolution of Logistics Thought," *Journal of Business Logistics,* Vol. 18, No. 2, 1997, pp. 15–29.

[2]John Paul MacDuffie and Susan Helper, "Creating Lean Suppliers: Diffusing Lean Production through the Supply Chain," *California Management Review,* Vol. 39, No. 4, 1997, pp. 118–151.

[3]Ibid.

[4]Lisa H. Harrington, "Supply Chain Integration from the Inside," *Transportation & Distribution,* March 1997, pp. 35–38.

[5]Op Cit. 2.

[6]Marc Berlow, "For Superb Supplier Development—Honda Wins," *Purchasing,* September 21, 1995, pp. 32–40.

[7]Ibid.

[8]Op Cit. 2

[9]Op Cit. 2

[10]Op Cit. 6

[11]Op Cit. 6

[12]Gillian Wolf, *International Directory of Company Histories,* Chicago: St. James Press, 1995.

[13]Ibid.

[14]http://www.harris.com/harris/chairmansmessage.html, 8–25–98

[15]Douglas F. Carlberg, "The Evolution of a World Class Factory at Harris Farinon," *National Productivity Review,* Vol. 15, No. 4, 1996, pp. 77–85.

[16]The Harris Corporation. (1994, August). *Annual Report.* Melbourne, FL.

[17]http://www.gap.com/com/company/aboutgap.asp, 05/26/98

[18]Nina Munk, "Gap Gets It," *Fortune,* August 3, 1998, pp. 68–82.

[19]Robert Mottley, "How The Gap Fills its Gaps in Logistics," *American Shipper,* January 1997, pp. 36–39.

[20]Becton Dickinson (1996). *Annual Report.* Franklin Lakes, NJ: Author.

[21]Ibid

[22]Ibid

[23]Lisa H. Harrington, "Supply Chain Integration from the Inside," *Transportation & Distribution,* March 1997, pp. 35–38

[24]Ibid

[25]Becton Dickinson (1996). *Annual Report.* Franklin Lakes, NJ: Author.

[26]Op. Cit. 23

[27]Op. Cit. 23

[28]Op. Cit. 23

[29]Op. Cit. 23

[30]Chris Gillis, "Centralized Management," *American Shipper,* January 1997, pp. 22–24.

[31]Mitchell E. MacDonald (1994), "How Johnson & Johnson Built its World-Class Program," *Traffic Management,* March, pp. 38–40.

■ CHAPTER 4

[1]Noel P. Greis and John D. Kasarda, "Enterprise Logistics in the Information Era," *California Management Review,* Vol. 39, No. 3, Spring 1997, p. 57.

[2]Frank Casale, "Strategic Outsourcing," *The Outsourcing Institute: 1996 Trends Report,* The Outsourcing Institute, New York, New York, 1996.

[3]Edward J. Bardi and Michael Tracey, "Transportation Outsourcing: A Survey of U.S. Practices," *International Journal of Physical Distribution and Logistics Management,* Vol. 21, No. 3, pp. 15–21, 1991.

[4]Bernard J. LaLonde and Martha C. Cooper, "Partnerships in Providing Customer Service: A Third Party Perspective," Council of Logistics Management, Oak Brook, Illinois, 1989.

[5]Bernard J. LaLonde and Arnold B. Maltz, "Some Propositions about Outsourcing the Logistics Function," *International Journal of Logistics Management,* Vol. 3, No. 1, pp. 1–11, 1992

[6]Robert C. Lieb, "The Use of Third Party Logistics by Large American Manufacturers," Journal of Business Logistics, Vol. 13, No. 2, pp. 29–42, Fall 1992.

[7]"A Shipper's Approach to Contract Logistics," A. T. Kearney, 1996, Chicago, Illinois.

[8]Chris Gillis, "Centralized Management: Johnson & Johnson Resists the Trend to Outsource Logistics Services to Third-Party Providers," American Shipper, January 1997, pp. 22–24.

[9]Outsourced Logistics Report, Volume 2, No. 3, March 31, 1996, pp. 1–3.

[10]Ibid.

[11]Outsourced Logistics Report, Vol. 1, No. 9, December 31, 1995, pp. 1–3.

[12]Outsourced Logistics Report, Vol. 2, No. 9, September 30, 1996, pp. 5.

[13]Robert C. Lieb, Robert A. Millen, and Luk Van Wassenhove, "Third-Party Logistics Services: A Comparison of Experienced American and European Manufacturers," International Journal of Physical Distribution & Logistics Management, Vol. 23, No. 6, 1993, p. 41.

[14]Robert C. Lieb and Hugh L. Randall, "A Comparison of the Use of Third-Party Logistics Services by Large American Manufacturers, 1991, 1994, and 1995" Journal of Business Logistics, Vol. 17, No. 1, 1996, p. 314.

■ CHAPTER 5

[1]University of Maryland, Supply Chain Management Center, "Outsourcing to Third Party Logistics Providers as an Emerging Management Option," September 24, 1997.

[2]The information in the database had two important drawbacks. First, there were multiple names from some organizations. Approximately 25 percent of the names had at least one other potential respondent from the same organization. Second, some managers had to be excluded since they worked for organizations not likely to use third party providers or for third party providers themselves.

[3]Very few (less than 20) surveys were returned to the researchers with an unknown addressee.

[4]Note that the true population of outsourcers is represented by the number of companies in the United States (or the world!) engaged in logistics outsourcing. Therefore, our sample size (463), as a ratio of the true population of outsourcers is larger than that obtained (to the best of our knowledge) by researchers in any other outsourcing study.

[5]Fifteen percent of the firms in our sample have between 1,000 and 2,499 employees, while 36.3 percent have 2,500 or more employees. Corresponding percentages from the population were 9.2 percent and 5.8 percent, respectively.

■ CHAPTER 6

[1]Michael E. Porter, "Competitive Advantage: Creating and Sustaining Superior Performance," New York Free Press, 1985.

■ CHAPTER 7

[1]K. Liebfried and C. McNair, "Benchmarking: A Tool for Continuous Improvement," New York: Harper Collins, 1992, pp. 59–60.

[2]R. Hayes and G. Pisana, "Beyond World Class: The New Manufacturing Strategy," *Harvard Business Review,* January-February 1994, pp. 77–86.

[3]Ibid.

Index